D0772358

FROM A TALLER TOWER

The Rise of the American Mass Shooter

SEAMUS MCGRAW

UNIVERSITY OF TEXAS PRESS

Austin

Requests for permission to reproduce material from this work should
be sent to:
    Permissions
    University of Texas Press
    P.O. Box 7819
    Austin, TX 78713-7819
    utpress.utexas.edu/rp-form

♾ The paper used in this book meets the minimum requirements of
ANSI/NISO Z39.48-1992 (R1997) (Permanence of Paper).

Library of Congress Cataloging-in-Publication Data

Names: McGraw, Seamus, author.
Title: From a taller tower : the rise of the American mass shooter /
    Seamus McGraw.
Description: First edition. | Austin : University of Texas Press, 2021. |
    Includes index.
Identifiers: LCCN 2020034081
    ISBN 978-1-4773-1718-1 (cloth)
    ISBN 978-1-4773-2263-5 (library ebook)
    ISBN 978-1-4773-2264-2 (non-library ebook)
Subjects: LCSH: Mass shootings—United States. | School shootings—
    United States. | Massacres—United States.
Classification: LCC HV6536.5.U6 M34 2021 | DDC 364.152/340973—
    dc23
LC record available at https://lccn.loc.gov/2020034081

doi:10.7560/317181

CONTENTS

Author's Note

I COMES OUT of nowhere, this random act of unspeakable violence. Not twenty feet away from me, a man—an indigent, timid, harmless wino but a man nonetheless—is being savagely bludgeoned nearly to death. And for what seems to be an eternity, I just stand there. Mute. Motionless. Helpless.

Useless.

I freeze. There is no other word for it.

It's not the way I imagined I would react had I ever conjured a scene of such brutality. I've always thought of myself as a bit of a hardass—if not exactly heroic, at least brave enough and tough enough to step in and do something. Anything. We all imagine ourselves to be heroes in waiting, I suppose. Until we're tested. But never in my wildest imagination had I dreamed up an image of an attack as senseless, as raw, as savage as this one.

It's the week between Christmas and New Year's in the winter of 1978. I'm all of nineteen, and I'm heading back to my home in central New Jersey from an evening on the town in New York. As usual, I've been drinking. And as usual, I've missed the last connecting train from Penn Station Newark to points south. It isn't the first time I've missed the train and will have to spend the night sobering up in the sooty, seedy old marble lobby of the terminal in Newark, waiting for the first train out in the morning. The nineteen-year-old me drinks a lot, and he misses a lot of things, trains included.

There's a cadre of regulars, ten or twelve guys who haunt the train station when all the decent types are home abed. I know a few of them by sight and one or two of them by name. Or by nickname. One of them is this harmless old wino, a man in his sixties, perhaps, who had earned the nickname "Bojangles." I assume he's called Bojangles because anytime I ever see him, winter or summer, he's wearing a stained and ragged black overcoat upon which he has tied and safety-pinned and otherwise fastened all his worldly possessions, everything from a gaudy ring full of keys to nothing in particular to a discarded folding baby stroller. Whenever he moves, usually using the wall as a support, he makes the most awful clattering racket. It echoes against the marble walls. I don't recall ever hearing him speak, but you always know when Bojangles is coming. You can hear him from across the concourse, and when he passes near you, slowly, painfully, he usually casts his bloodshot and yellow eyes downward, a signal that he means no one any harm.

It's about three in the morning when the heavy glass and brushed steel door on the east side of the concourse swings open, and a gust of frigid air stinking of diesel exhaust rushes in, and with it a tightly muscled man with a freshly shaved head who appears to be in his early thirties. He immediately catches my attention, in part because of his appearance and his dress—he's wildly underdressed for the cold winter night, wearing only a pair of light slacks and a light-colored V-neck sweater— but also for the purposeful, serious way he struts into the station. He's carrying what appears to be a walking stick, though it clanks with a metallic sound that echoes against the marble with his every step. Even now, all these years later, I can still hear the echo of it. He has a rigid gait, the self-consciously aggressive strut of a man who thinks himself important, a man who demands with every step that you too see him as someone to be reckoned with, a man in a hurry to get someplace, even if that place is a train station in Newark in the middle of the night, filled with people who aren't going anywhere anytime soon.

He strides past me, his walking stick clanking, and goes no more than ten or fifteen paces when he reaches the spot along the wall where Bojangles is staggering. He stops abruptly. He turns. And for the space of a heartbeat, he just glares at Bojangles. He does not know the man, I'll later learn. He's never spoken with him, and Bojangles has certainly never given him any offense. He's never given anyone any offense that I'm aware of. But there's rage and fury in the bald-headed man's eyes.

And then, without warning, without provocation, he lunges toward Bojangles, raising his walking stick, which I now see is an iron bar. Before the first blow lands, Bojangles finally looks up. There's terror in his eyes. And pleading. That means nothing to the bald-headed man. Again and again in a furious barrage of blows, he strikes Bojangles with the iron bar. Blood splatters. Broken teeth skitter across the marble floor toward where I am standing.

I'm no more than twenty feet away from Bojangles and his attacker. I could close the distance between us in the space between the blows. But I'm frozen where I stand. Mute. Motionless. Helpless. Useless. And I'm not the only one. All the other late-night denizens of the Newark train station, who no doubt imagine themselves to be hard-asses too, are frozen as well, watching without under-standing, staring in stunned horror as this innocent, harmless old man is savaged. It seems like an eternity. In truth it's maybe thirty seconds, forty-five at the most, before out of the corner of my eye, I see one of the deni-zens flinch, and that's enough to jar me from my stupor. Almost as one, all of us, the regulars, lunge toward the bald-headed man, and he backs away, waving the iron bar at us and bellowing something unintelligible. For the next few minutes we hold him at bay, feinting toward him as if we're baiting an animal, until police finally arrive and take him into custody.

But by that point, the damage is done. A harmless old man is critically injured in an act of irrational, wan-ton bloodlust. He will survive, though he will carry the scars—physical and, I'm sure, psychological—of that attack for the rest of his life. And so will everyone else who was there that night.

For years afterward, I tortured myself for my inac-tion that night. I called myself a coward, and if I'm to be honest, I still haven't completely absolved myself for the awful sin of omission I committed. Indeed, to this day I am still compensating for what I didn't do instinc-tively that night. I'm in my sixties and I still take reckless chances sometimes, at least in part to convince myself that I am not a coward.

But a larger part of me now understands, with the help of time and the wisdom of others, that it was some-thing more than just fear that made me, and the others in that terminal, freeze.

Certainly, fear was part of it. But I was no less fearful when the others and I finally did shake off our stupor and rush the attacker. No, the reason I froze that night was more than fear—or less. Psychologists tell us that there are two primary responses to danger: we either flee, or we fight. But in order for our limbic system to trigger either of those two responses, they tell us, we must first process the atrocity that is occurring in front of us, if only in the most primitive part of our brain. We must recognize it and assess it. But what happens when a scene of such unexpected savagery and brutality erupts right before your eyes, an act of violence so extreme, so utterly, unimaginably random that nothing in your experience has ever prepared you for it? In my case, literally nothing happened: for thirty or forty-five precious seconds that could have meant the difference between life and death for an innocent man, I simply shut down, unable to find any analogue to the bloody scene that was playing out before me that would signal which of those two primal responses I should choose. My response was to do nothing.

I froze. There is no other word for it.

I've revisited that scene in my mind a hundred times or more as I've been working on this book. I've thought about it in the context of those who've survived mass public atrocities and those who didn't. It was very much in my mind as I spoke with first responders who found themselves thrust into the center of events that were more horrific than anything they'd ever experienced. And I've considered it in the context of those heroic individuals, armed and unarmed, who—unlike me—did not hesitate to rush in and do something to stop them. I've measured their actions against my own that night, and I have found myself wanting.

So be it.

But perhaps more important, I've also considered it in the context of our larger societal response, or lack thereof, to the mounting casualty count of what can now best be described as an epidemic of mass public shootings. If it's true, as psychologist and trauma survivor Roger Friedman tells us in chapter 9, that the contours of our own personal traumas can be seen on a grand scale in society at large, then perhaps that explains why, in the wake of each new mass public shooting, we seem to be frozen as a people. Mute. Motionless. Helpless.

For more than fifty years now, from the massacre at the University of Texas in 1966 to the mass murder from the Mandalay Bay hotel in Las Vegas and beyond, we as a nation have stood largely silent as these atrocities have been committed. We have failed to stop them or even to take significant steps to make them less likely.

I don't know what it will take to shake us from our stupor. But, as we'll examine in the epilogue, if you look out of the corner of your eye, it's possible that at last we're seeing the first slight movements that might jar us into action. It's not enough. But it's something.

There is, perhaps, reason for cautious hope in that.

There is one other point I need to make. The reader may find some of the language in this book jarring, particularly as it relates to my characterizations of the killers, and especially with regard to the murderer who killed dozens of Muslim worshippers in Christchurch, New Zealand. I confess that I have in some cases abandoned the careful, measured, neutral tone that journalists are trained to use when describing such people and events. There's a reason for that. Several analysts and experts I have spoken to have told me that neutral language can distort rather than illuminate the actions and motivations of these killers. That dispassionate language, they've told me, can open a way for those who are so inclined to create myths around these murderers, turning them into perverse folk heroes in some of the darker corners of our culture. I'm not naïve enough to imagine that this book is going to impede that to any great degree. But I do believe that it is important to strip away any ambiguity and to present a more precise and accurate—and, yes, emotionally charged—description of these killers, to present them as the cruel narcissists that they are.

Finally, I know with absolute certainty that despite my efforts to keep from sensationalizing these crimes, my depictions of some of the atrocities will reopen old wounds and cause immense pain to people who have suffered far more than you or I ever have or hopefully ever will.

It was my call to do it, and I take full responsibility for the consequences of every word that's in this book.

I also take full responsibility for the words that are not in it.

There are two of those. The first is "tragedy"—the go-to word after every one of these massacres. Tragedies are mythic, beyond human control. These are not tragedies. These are atrocities. These are things we do. To each other.

The second is "victim," at least as it relates to those who have been murdered in this epidemic of violence. Victimhood is a choice, and "victim" is a word many of these killers perversely appropriate for themselves. The survivors I've spoken to and the families of those who didn't survive by and large don't see themselves or their lost loved ones as victims.

And neither do I.

I see them as heroes.

And this book is for them.

FROM A
TALLER
TOWER

The Deepest Silence There Is

There is no silence on earth deeper than the silence between gunshots. It's terrifying. It's deafening. It drowns out everything else.

The shooting had become sporadic now, the awful crack of a rifle round, a puff of white gun smoke drifting up from behind the chalky white ramparts of the observation deck on the twenty-eighth floor of the Tower, followed by a chaotic barrage from the cops and the armed civilians below. Maybe after all these years, his memory is playing tricks on him, but he remembers watching as limestone dust rose from the spots their bullets hit and then dissipated into the empty blue of a hot August sky.[1]

For a moment or two, there'd be silence. And then the shooting would begin again.

There is no silence on earth deeper than the silence between gunshots. It's deafening. It drowns out everything else. Even your sense of humanity, he thought.

Somewhere deep inside, the young cop felt it, the stab of compassion for the wounded, for the dying, for the dead. He felt it when he looked into the eyes of that young woman, seven months pregnant. The gunman's first round from the Tower ripped through her pelvis and killed the baby boy inside her. The next instantly killed her boyfriend. He fell atop her.

Decades later she'd remember the pain, and she'd remember the awful relentless heat; she'd remember the deep and deathly stillness in her womb and how that silence inside her seemed to be spilling out like blood, a silence that would pool around her for the rest of her life. She'd remember how that silence silenced her when she returned to school the following year, silenced her friends, even her husband, who could not help but notice the scar and the depression on her body where the gunman's bullet had shattered her iliac crest, but who never once asked about it. There is no silence on earth deeper than the silence between gunshots, and sometimes, it lasts a lifetime. She could not move. Nor speak. She just lay there—writhing in anguish, fear, pain, and, above all, confusion.[2]

All that training he'd had in the army as a medic, the young cop had to choke that back. Even if he had been prepared for an atrocity like this—even if he had a pack full of bandages and all the tools needed to render aid—there was no time. The killing had been going on for nearly an hour and a half. There were thirty-one wounded. There were already eleven dead on the ground, if you counted the baby killed inside the young woman's womb. The young cop's colleague, an Austin patrolman named Billy Paul Speed, was among them. Three more were dead inside the Tower. Two others there were wounded.

It wouldn't be until hours later that police would find two more dead, across town. In the hours before dawn, before he headed to the campus, the mass murderer had stabbed his mother to death, claiming in his self-serving suicide note that he was doing her a kindness by sparing her what was to come. He then drove home and murdered his wife. That made sixteen, though decades after the shooting ended a seventeenth person would finally succumb to injuries suffered that day. There'd have been more, certainly, if the gunman hadn't been stopped.

It wasn't a fully formed thought, or even an order that someone had once given him, remembered and then retrieved in the chaos of the moment. It was more like an instinct.

It could be distilled into this:

Stop the killing, then stop the dying.

No one had ever told him that. No one had ever given him that order. No one had ever thought to. No one had ever trained for this kind of atrocity because until that very moment, no one could ever have imagined that such a thing could happen. There had been mass murders in America before. Our history is steeped in mass violence. But this was something different. Deadly. Random. Utterly inexplicable.

The horror of it all was not confined that day to the "Forty Acres" around the base of the Tower at the University of Texas. All the technological advancements of modern American life had come together by August 1, 1966, and the mass killing—what we would come to think of as the first "mass public shooting"—was being broadcast live across the state, across the nation. This was a national trauma, and out of it, soon enough, we would fashion a canon of myths and misconceptions that we'd hope—futilely—would explain how such a thing could happen, even as those same myths would continue to inflame scores of mass public shooters in the decades to come.

But at that moment, no one, least of all Ramiro

Martinez, the young Austin cop, could think that far ahead.

Stop the killing, then stop the dying.

He knew it intuitively at his core: he had no choice but to leave the young woman there. Someday he'd see her again. He'd learn her name. Claire Wilson. And he'd learn the name of her dead boyfriend. Tom Eckman. The baby would never get a name. Someday he'd get a chance to tell her how sorry he was that he had left her there. Someday. But not today.

He made his way to the base of the Tower, zigzagging to cheat the sniper's sights. He found his way inside. It was cool and dark. A security guard, as frightened and confused as Martinez was, had been unable to raise anybody on his two-way radio. Martinez took it from him and tried to call in reinforcements himself. He couldn't get through either. The communications system used by the Austin police was no match for the madness that was taking place. It had not been designed to handle this much chaos. Too many frantic voices jammed the channels.

And so Martinez whispered an Act of Contrition to himself and rode the elevator to the twenty-sixth floor, making the sign of the cross with one hand and holding his .38 in the other. He would not be alone up there. Officer Houston McCoy, a laconic cowboy of a man, and a heroic civilian named Allen Crum—who had asked to be deputized on the spot—were barreling up the stairs toward the killer's perch.

The stench of burnt powder and blood and death saturated the air when the elevator doors opened. Once again Martinez hurried past the dying and the dead. Behind a desk in a little reception room lay the body of receptionist Edna Elizabeth Townsley, a diminutive woman with a loud and infectious laugh who had been the first person murdered when the killer entered the Tower. Not far beyond her, near the two flights of steps to the observation area, he passed the bodies of Martin "Mark" Gabour and Marguerite Lamport, who had been killed with a blast from the murderer's sawed-off shotgun. And not far from them, Gabour's brother, Mike, and their mother, Mary, both wounded, played dead until the makeshift posse arrived.

"Let me shoot the son of a bitch," the young man had said as he reached for the shotgun in McCoy's hands. "I'll shoot him for you," McCoy said.

And then it was back out into the relentless August heat, the relentless sun, the pale blue Austin sky, and deep into what veterans of bloodshed refer to as the fog of war.

We will never know for sure what happened in those next few fraught moments on the observation deck at the University of Texas on that first day of August in 1966. We'll never be able to say with absolute certainty who fired the rounds that ultimately brought the killer down. Recollections of those involved in such moments are almost always unreliable.

We do know that both McCoy and Martinez confronted the killer as Crum eased around the parapet from the other direction. We know that the killer was ready for them. He laid down the Remington 700—a hunting rifle that carries a certain mystique among a certain breed of shooter who fantasizes about being a sniper. He reached into the footlocker he had carted up the elevator with him; it held Spam sandwiches and sweet rolls, canned food and tins of evaporated milk, rope, an extension cord, binoculars, a toy compass, and a small arsenal that included the 12-gauge shotgun he had used to murder Townsley, two pistols, an ammunition box, and a brand spanking new M-1 carbine, a weapon that as a Marine he had been trained to use in close combat. He had just purchased the shotgun and the M-1, apparently in preparation for the crimes he was about to commit.

He reached for the M-1.

It's strange. All these years later, we can conjure—not always accurately—an image of a mass public shooter, and that image looks a lot like the killer in the Tower that day: a young white man full of rage over some imagined injustice done to him. But Martinez and McCoy and Crum had no such mythological image in their minds. It had not yet been planted in the American psyche. All they saw was body mass and an M-1, and they did what they came to do.

They had to keep low. Bullets from the cops and well-meaning civilians below—some had rushed home to fetch their hunting rifles—screeched over their heads and bored their way into the limestone of the Tower.

McCoy let loose a blast from his shotgun as Martinez emptied the chamber of his .38. McCoy's blast peppered the killer's skull with pellets. One of Martinez's bullets splintered the stock on the killer's assault rifle. The killer slumped to the floor of the observation deck, but he was still moving, still alive. So Martinez grabbed McCoy's shotgun out of his hand and fired again at close range. The killer stopped moving.

Before they buried the killer in a casket draped with the American flag—once a Marine, always a Marine[3]— at a cemetery about half an hour's drive from Parkland, Florida, which in time would become infamous for its own massacre, they performed an autopsy. The autopsy didn't reveal much. The killer had already been embalmed before the medical examiner ever got a chance to unwrap his scalpel. But it did conclusively show that he had been hit by at least one bullet, presumably from Martinez's .38, and by pellets from McCoy's shotgun.

Martinez raised the shotgun over his head and waved it, as a signal to the shooters below. "We got him!" he screamed. But they didn't hear him. Then he let the full terrible weight of what had just happened overcome him. He sank to the floor, telling himself that he had done what he had gone there to do.

Stop the killing. For now.

Stop the dying. For now.

Eventually, the firing from below petered out, and there was silence. There is no deeper silence on earth than the silence between gunshots. It's deafening.

* * *

His name was Charles Joseph Whitman.

There. I've said it. And it will be the last time his name will be mentioned in this book. If there is a contagion in this country, and in those countries that take their cues from our culture, if there is a virulent epidemic of mass, irrational violence in this nation—and there is—then the gunman who murdered seventeen people in Texas on August 1, 1966, is Patient Zero.

We've made him mythic. We've granted him and those who have followed his path through the next six bloody decades—from the parking lot of the Cleveland School in San Diego to the library in Columbine High School to a synagogue in Pittsburgh and a mosque in Christchurch, New Zealand—a status none of them deserve.

We tell ourselves that this murderer was the all-American boy, the boy next door, an Eagle Scout, a clean-cut Marine, a guy just like the rest of us, only more so.

The supreme tragedy is that in some regards it's absolutely true, and our shame is the greater for it.

The gunman at the parapet in Austin was certainly not the first mass murderer in American history, nor was this the first time a cold-blooded killer had massacred strangers. This wasn't even the first mass slaying during the summer of 1966. Just nineteen days earlier, sometime after eleven p.m. on the night of July 13, a drunken and drug-addled merchant marine who had been raised in Texas by a criminal stepfather had slipped into a rooming house at 2319 East 100th Street in Chicago.

Over the course of the next eight hours, he strangled and stabbed (and in at least one case raped) eight student nurses one by one, until only one, who had hidden in terror beneath a bed, survived. For nearly three weeks the evening news and the pages of America's newspapers were filled with the awful, lurid details of the murderous orgy. The killer's name—Speck, a synonym for an insignificant mote of filth—would become a household word; his gaunt, pockmarked face would be as familiar to millions of Americans as any movie star's or sports hero's. Soon enough, within days really, this killer would be deposed as America's worst nightmare, just as every mass killer since would be. The last to be killed by every mass killer is always the mass killer who came before.

But as shocking as the mass murder in the rooming house was, that killer was at least darkly familiar to us, in a perverse way. The news stories portrayed him as a figure drawn from our nightmares, a monster with tentacles that reached deep into our mythology. He looked like a monster; he had lived monstrously. All of our theology—sectarian and secular—is and always has been shot through with cautionary tales of such monsters acting on the most animalistic impulses. Monsters are by definition different from us, we tell ourselves. And because they're different, for all the horror they inflict, they also do one great kindness. They absolve us of complicity. And sometimes we return the favor, granting mass murderers not just absolution but honor.

As far back as the colonial era, there have been gruesome mass killings. The slaying of the surviving members of the Susquehannock Indian tribe in revenge for the predations of Pontiac's warriors during the French and Indian War, carried out by a murderous band of vigilante colonists who called themselves the Paxton Boys, is just one example.

The Paxton Boys were seen as heroes by some at the time. A hundred miles to the northeast of that stretch of Pennsylvania, along the banks of the Delaware River, there's still a monument to the "Indian Fighter" Tom Quick. An old inn named for him still graces the tree-lined main street of Milford, Pennsylvania. It's directly across the street from the courthouse where, two and a half centuries later, one of his spiritual descendants, another murderer who also portrayed himself as a warrior, would be tried for gunning down two state policemen in a sneak attack.

Among Quick's glorious exploits was the murder of a mother and her three young children as they cowered together in the rushes along the river. "Nits make lice," he is rumored to have said in defense of his act of infanticide.[4] And that was good enough to earn him a minor place in the pantheon of American frontiersmen.

On other occasions we even romanticize the killings, turning brutal killers like Clyde Barrow and Bonnie Parker or the murderous machine gunners who executed seven members of Bugs Moran's gang in a Chicago garage on February 14, 1929, into Hollywood-ized icons. We continue to do so today, even as we meekly decry the gang and gun violence in Chicago and other American cities. Gun-toting gangsters are often still our go-to antiheroes. Even now it still hasn't quite dawned on us that by mythologizing the first St. Valentine's Day Massacre, we may have helped bring about the second St. Valentine's Day Massacre, the one on February 14, 2018, when a teen armed with a military-style rifle murdered seventeen people at a Florida high school and wounded seventeen more.

But on that first day of August 1966, the killer in Austin robbed us of those comforting myths. We could no longer pretend that the monsters didn't look or act like us. We could no longer excuse them because they were killing somebody whom, unjust though it may have been, we officially sanctioned as an adversary. The atrocity committed in Austin that day was a turning point in our history. It was arguably the first truly modern mass public shooting, perpetrated by a killer who at first glance seems indistinguishable from those he killed. He committed murder on a grand scale, not to advance some perverse but comprehensible criminal enterprise or in obvious service to some equally perverse imagined cause, but instead for no discernible reason. It was the first in a seemingly endless series of senseless mass shootings whose frequency has risen and fallen over the decades but that now seem to be happening more often and with far higher death tolls. The Tower murders would demand that we concoct new myths to explain the killing. And we would oblige. But even those new myths, in the end, would always be swallowed by the silence.

The silence between gunshots, that deafening and deadly silence, is as deep as ever. But it no longer lasts very long at all.

CHAPTER 1

The Texas
Sharpshooter
Fallacy

There was a rumor
about a tumor
nestled at the base of his brain . . .
Laughing wildly as he bagged them
Who are we to say the boy's insane?

Kinky Friedman

THERE WERE, ACCORDING to the *Vital Statistics of the United States*, 14,170 deaths linked to tumors in Texas in 1966.[1] But there is no evidence that even one of those deaths occurred on the University of Texas campus on the first day of August that year, nor in the cramped Austin apartment the killer shared with his wife before he murdered her in her sleep, nor in his mother's apartment where she too was slain.

Indeed, there is no conclusive evidence that any of the seventeen people who were murdered that day died as a result of a tumor. Not theirs, not the killer's.

And yet, even now, five decades and counting after the murders, a great many people still take it as an article of faith that a pecan-sized tumor nestled between the killer's thalamus, hypothalamus, and amygdala—the last one, the portion of the brain that controls emotions and behavior—was somehow the cause of all the bloodshed.

It is, perhaps, understandable that so many people still point to the killer's tumor as a possible factor driving him to carry out the atrocity he committed. After all, even the Connally Commission—a blue-ribbon panel of giant brains, neurosurgeons and psychiatrists among them, who studied every aspect of the massacre—could not conclusively rule out that the tumor played a role. They sliced the killer's brain, placed it on slides like some kind of grotesque miniature monstrance, and studied it under a microscope. They found evidence of the tumor, though there are some still today who dispute that the damaged tissue proved its existence conclusively. They allowed that it might explain the excruciating headaches the killer wrote about in his obsessively meticulous diary. But whether it—or some other pathology that couldn't be measured in centimeters and weighed in grams—was the root of what the killer himself described in his diary as his "many unusual and irrational thoughts" remains an open question.

The commissioners wrote, in a section of the report that has been widely reprinted, that the tumor "conceivably could have contributed to his inability to control his emotions and his actions" before concluding, with a virtual shrug of their shoulders, that "the application of existing knowledge of organic brain function does not enable us to explain the actions of [the killer] on August first."[2]

And it would be almost comforting to imagine that there was one, easily identifiable cause that could explain the malevolence that was unleashed that day. Maybe if we could find the first cause of that first modern mass public shooting, we might hope that we could find the first cause of all the massacres that have followed.

If only it were that easy.

If only the malignancy could be spotted on an X-ray or a CT scan, then we could send in teams of surgeons to cut it out. We could be done with it. But mass shootings, even in the term's narrowest definition—a single event in which at least four people are killed, not counting the gunman, that is unrelated to crime or overtly political motives—have killed at least 1,203 Americans since the Tower massacre.[3]

And excising it is not that easy.

Because whatever invisible malignancy afflicts these murderers, it seems to have metastasized in us as well. We are, as a nation, among the most violence-prone people on earth, both against others and against ourselves. An estimated 15,129 murders were committed in the United States in 2017 (the last year for which FBI statistics are available), not to mention the 47,173 suicides that year. (Suicide numbers have been increasing in the United States for the last twenty years even as global suicide rates have declined.) These numbers have earned us the distinction among developed nations as the place where you're most likely to meet a violent end.[4]

It's not that our crime rate is any higher than those elsewhere in the first world. As Franklin Zimring and Gordon Hawkins note in their book *Crime Is Not the Problem* (1997), a treatise that has remained remarkably durable over the years, our rates of common property crimes are well within the norm for affluent countries.[5]

Our body count is not. But why?

It may be partly because we are a technologically proficient people who are simply better equipped to kill and maim. Of those murders in 2017, 72.6 percent were committed with firearms.[6] More than half of all the suicides committed in this country that year were committed with guns.[7] We are, as has often been pointed out, awash in firearms in America. About 40 percent of all the privately owned small arms in the world belong to

Americans, according to the Swiss-based Small Arms Survey. There are an estimated 393 million guns, according to the government's 2018 SAS report, in a country of 329 million people, or 120.5 firearms for every one hundred people.[8]

That's one gun for every man, woman, and child in America, with enough left over to give one to everyone in Canada and Australia if we were feeling generous and they didn't have such rigorous gun regulations. But not every man, woman, and child in America owns a gun. In fact, as of 2014, only about 31 percent of Americans lived in a household that owns firearms, and gun ownership has generally declined over the past forty years.[9] It's just that those who still cling to them cling to them by the armload.

Our records are incomplete. But according to the National Shooting Sports Foundation, about 8.5 million of those weapons manufactured or imported into the United States between 1990 and 2012 are so-called "modern sporting rifles," among them the lightweight, semiautomatic, rapid-fire spiritual descendants of the M-1 the killer carried with him up the Tower that day so long ago in Austin.[10] This class of weapons can easily be fitted with extended magazines, enabling even the least competent shooter to squeeze off two rounds a second for the eight to ten minutes it can often take for police to respond to a 911 call about shots fired. As many as two million more weapons have been manufactured or imported every year since 2012, according to the nonprofit news organization the Trace, founded by seed money from the gun control advocacy group Everytown for Gun Safety.[11]

It is true, as gun rights advocates so often point out, that such weapons are rarely used to commit crimes. Although it's admittedly an incomplete accounting, according to the FBI's 2017 Uniform Crime Report (UCR), if you were the target of an aggravated assault that year, it was three times more likely that your attacker would have come at you with a knife, a blunt object, or his bare hands than with a firearm of any description, let alone a semiautomatic rifle or handgun.[12]

But when an active shooter—and it is most often a male—does get his hands on a semiautomatic rifle, the results are catastrophic. According to a 2018 report compiled by Brigham and Women's Hospital and published in the *Journal of the American Medical Association*, active shooters armed with any kind of semiautomatic rifle are likely to kill or wound nearly twice as many people as killers armed with firearms that fire off far fewer rounds before needing to be reloaded.[13]

Just ask the twenty-six people who were shot with a semiautomatic rifle at Sandy Hook Elementary School in Connecticut in 2012, most of them children, most of them slain in the first seven minutes of the massacre by a killer who had first shot his mother to death. Or the thirty-four people who were killed or wounded by a shooter at Marjory Stoneman Douglas High School in Parkland, Florida, on Valentine's Day 2018. Or the 471 people who were shot five months later when a killer with an arsenal of semiautomatic weapons, perched in a hotel high-rise and situated a hundred feet higher than the University of Texas shooter, rained gunfire on a crowd of country music fans in Las Vegas. You can ask them. But 102 of the people targeted by those killers are no longer alive to answer.

And what of semiautomatic handguns, like the ones used when a gunman killed eleven people at a nightclub in Thousand Oaks, California, in November 2018, or the Glock 19 and the Walther P22 a student used to murder thirty-two people and wound seventeen more at Virginia Tech in 2007, or the silencer-equipped handgun used to kill eleven municipal workers and a private contractor trying to obtain a permit at a municipal building in Virginia Beach, Virginia, in June 2019? There's no telling how many weapons like those are privately owned in the United States. Records are incomplete. We do know that handguns of every description accounted for nearly half (46.4 percent) of the murders committed in the United States in 2017.[14] We also know that about 5.5 million new pistols and revolvers were manufactured in 2016, according to figures compiled by the federal Bureau of Alcohol, Tobacco, Firearms and Explosives,[15] and in recent years at least two-thirds of the handguns entering the market have been semiautomatics.[16]

We are indeed a nation awash in guns. Throughout our history they have been both a tool and a talisman, says David Snyder, now a professor of history at Delaware Valley University in Pennsylvania, who has had a long-standing interest in gun violence ever since one of his former students murdered dozens at his old school in Virginia. Throughout our history, guns have been a totem of independence for some folks, usually white males, he says. Indeed, it was at least in part to protect the privileges of white slave owners in the early days of our country that the Second Amendment was written, says Snyder. And as we'll see in chapter 8, the precious right to bear arms is, for many Americans, not just a civil sacrament; in some quarters it's been invested with a religious significance—a belief that gun ownership is a natural right derived from heaven.

In times of stress, personal or public, firearms are often what many Americans turn to for a sense of security. It's no surprise that in March 2020, when a deadly pandemic spread across the country and the world, when most of the country was locked down and most of our shops and businesses were closed, gun stores in many places were considered essential businesses, and federal authorities reported doing a record 3.7 million background checks in that one month alone.[17] Similar but smaller spikes have been recorded after many moments of social disruption or in times of uncertainty and fear. Well before the coronavirus-fueled run on guns, America boasted the largest number of gun-toting residents in the developed world. And there is evidence that our easy access to firearms may be a significant factor in cementing our unenviable status when it comes to mass public shootings. According to a 2013 study of mass shootings at schools, churches, mosques, movie theaters, and workplaces, about a third of the active shooters in the world since that first mass public shooting at the University of Texas were active in the United States, even though we account for only 5 percent of the world's population.[18] The one variable that sets us apart, the study finds, is our staggeringly high rate of gun ownership, almost double the rate in any other nation.

But we are not the only nation with large numbers of firearms in private hands. Australia, Canada, and New Zealand all have at least a million firearms in circulation, yet their homicide rates are far lower than ours. Atrocities like the mass public shootings that have seemingly become routine in this country are rarer in those nations, and when they do occur—as happened in the bloody rampage by a murderer masquerading as a racial warrior and armed with several semiautomatic weapons who gunned down worshippers at two New Zealand mosques in March 2019—as often as not the killer pays homage to the darkest depths of American culture while at the same time trying to supplant American killers as the world's most terrible monster.

Even when these mass slayings occur elsewhere around the globe—in Norway or Quebec or Christchurch—there is something distinctly American about them.

Perhaps that's not surprising.

This is, after all, the country where the modern mass public shooter first materialized, and we are still, by far, the nation with the largest number of casualties resulting from those atrocities.

Certainly, the ease with which singularly efficient weapons can be obtained in the United States is a unique and significant factor contributing to the epidemic of gun violence in this country, say experts like David Chipman, a former agent with the Bureau of Alcohol, Tobacco, Firearms and Explosives and now a senior policy advisor for the organization known as Giffords Courage to Fight Gun Violence. But is it the only factor? Are there perhaps other aspects, peculiar to our history and our culture, that combine in a lethal, distinctly American cocktail— each element reinforcing the other—that makes us more vulnerable to these kinds of atrocities? Could it be that in our desperation to find a single silver bullet—whether it's guns or tumors or violent video games—that would explain away all the deadly lead ones, we are missing the big picture? Are we missing precious opportunities not just to reduce the number of mass public shootings, but to use what we could learn to save some of the thousands who die every year by their own hands, or at the hands of their spouses or partners, or at the hands of comparative strangers?

What research there is suggests that many of the same impulses and traits we find in mass public shooters are also frequently in evidence in men who kill their wives and children, and to some degree among those who put their guns to their own heads.

The phenomenon is called the Texas Sharpshooter Fallacy.

It's a concept used by statisticians to explain how easy it is to focus on a cluster of specific data points that support a particular, foregone conclusion while ignoring an equally significant number of data points that challenge it. It conjures the image of an imaginary marksman, looking at a target, counting his hits and ignoring his misses. It can, perhaps, be applied to one murderous sharpshooter in Texas in particular, and to our persistent desire to trace his bloody actions that day to a single, measurable—and by implication, correctable—cause.

But to do that we have to ignore other evidence.

Certainly, it's not entirely impossible that the tumor was at least one cause of what he himself described as his "irrational thoughts."

But how then do we explain the eminently rational steps he took over a couple of days to prepare for the attack? How do we explain the careful, detailed, and meticulous planning he carried out with almost military discipline, soberly acquiring everything he'd need to carry out the massacre and to gird himself for an anticipated siege by police?

Was it irrational that he had the cold-blooded presence of mind to even acquire a disguise—a pair of workman-like overalls and a hand truck—to escape detection before he began shooting?

As we've seen in the years since, these are the kinds of steps that have become so common among active shooters that the FBI, in its 2018 report "A Study of Pre-Attack Behaviors of Active Shooters in the United States, 2000–2013," devotes three full pages to the phenomenon. And few, if any, of the shooters whose behavior was evaluated were ever diagnosed with brain tumors.

Was it irrational for the murderer to point us toward his tumor in the first place, or could that also have been part of the same broader pathology that led to his rampage: an attempt to justify the atrocity he committed by claiming to be some kind of victim?

If we look more closely at the diaries and writings in which the murderer so directly urges us to examine his tumor, we find that in a much less deliberate and overtly manipulative way, they paint a far less sympathetic picture of the killer.

They paint a picture of a man author Gary Lavergne has described as a vain and preening gun-obsessed narcissist. Intelligent, yes, moderately, but psychologically fragile as well. So fragile that he couldn't bear it when the Marines decided that he wasn't the golden boy they had once imagined him to be. He had a hard time accepting the fact that the rules that applied to other people also applied to him, and he once found himself in a Marine brig for gambling and possession of an unauthorized handgun. The Marines dropped him from the program that was paying his tuition at the university. So fragile and self-absorbed was he that he blamed the Marines and the university—not himself, never himself—for his failure, Lavergne says.

His diaries, and the interviews reporters and writers have conducted over the years with those who thought they knew him, present the image of a selfish, drug-abusing man-child, the overbearing and self-absorbed son of a rigid, cold, and reportedly abusive father.

They paint a picture of a calculating chameleon of a man, a guy who, like other mass shooters to follow—the more outwardly aggressive of the two killers behind the Columbine massacre, for instance—could present one face to the world when he wanted to, and stare in self-reverential rapture at another, entirely different face in the mirror.

They paint a picture of a man with a streak of jealous misogyny that, as we will see in later chapters, has also been displayed by several other mass shooters who came after him.

He was a man who would hold his wife up to the world as some kind of prized possession, who could present himself as a loving and dutiful son to his mother, while at the same time seething over his dependence on them both.

As Lavergne, who wrote *A Sniper in the Tower*, the seminal book on the killer, put it in a recent conversation with me, "He could be a good son, until he wasn't. He could be a loving husband, and then he'd beat his wife."

Maybe it was just the terrible luck of the draw that the first three people he murdered that day were women, two of them the women closest to him in his life.

Maybe it was just chance that the first person this expert marksman carefully targeted through his four-power scope from the Tower that day was a young pregnant woman, and maybe it was just windage and chance that sent his bullet spiraling directly into her womb.

Then again, maybe it wasn't.

Those dark impulses—the narcissism, the rage, the misogyny, the sense of victimhood, and the obsession with some imagined injustice—had almost certainly begun to form in the killer's brain long before the tumor ever did.

They're the same dark impulses, as we'll see, that were evident in other mass public shooters who committed even bloodier atrocities over the next fifty-plus years, killers who were never diagnosed with a tumor. Indeed, as several researchers I spoke with contend, among them Casey Kelly, director of graduate studies and an associate professor of rhetoric and public culture at the University of Nebraska, these killers often harbor many of the same real or imagined grudges that have metastasized in much of American culture.

Yes, researchers tell us, we are a people awash in guns. Guns do kill people, and as we've seen, easily accessible, rapid-fire, high-capacity firearms kill people in larger numbers. As University of Alabama researcher and criminology professor Adam Lankford told me, across the world, "countries with higher firearms ownership rates among civilians were the countries where there were more public mass shootings."

But he adds, "Nowhere in the world compares to us in terms of firearms murder rates. We're more than double those other countries."

Why?

Is it that we are a people with a history of violence

and a mythology that celebrates it? Or is it that in our personal lives and in our national life, say experts like Lankford and Kelly, we have become inured to rage, have been beguiled by narcissism and seduced by a sense of victimhood?

Sociologists Bradley Campbell and Jason Manning have studied what they describe as a rising "culture of victimhood" that is bleeding across America. They see a culture in which it becomes almost a virtue to see yourself as aggrieved, injured, worthy of being granted compensation for that injury, and, when it's not granted, taking it anyway.[19]

That cultural embrace of victimhood is, in some regards, "a luxury," says Lankford. It can best take root in a society that is affluent enough to make grand promises—economic and social—to its children.

In other, less affluent nations, where there is less sense of entitlement, victimhood is considered a cause of shame, such as in so-called "honor societies" that prize dignity, Campbell and Manning write. In America, at least in some quarters, victimhood seems to grant status. As Kelly puts it, being injured in some obscure manner grants leave to some folks among us to explain away their personal failures or disappointments, blaming them on an often-vague Other—people of color, women, Jews, a coworker, or, as we've seen in some school shootings, the popular kids. In a world that increasingly exists online, there are plenty of virtual gathering places, as I'll explore in chapter 4, where those sentiments are shared and validated and indeed amplified.

It's an irony of our moment in history. As a nation we are becoming in many ways ever more isolated from each other even as we become more connected than ever before; a nation of people who don't know their next-door neighbors, but, thanks to mass and social media, know the most intimate details of the lives of complete strangers. Perhaps as a result, we've increasingly become a nation of people who crave notoriety. Fame. Infamy. It seems we no longer make the distinction. A study conducted by the Pew Research Center in 2007 found that one in ten young people between the ages of eighteen and twenty-five craved fame more than they craved anything else. For more than 40 percent, it was their second most fervent wish. Being leaders in their real, live, actual communities came in far below that, with only 7 percent saying it mattered to them.[20]

Maybe it's just a coincidence that the first modern mass public shooting was committed as America's mobile, postwar economic boom was reaching its apex, with all that it promised. Maybe it means nothing that the killer, a resentful, unsuccessful student at a major university, committed his crimes at one of the most iconic symbols of America's belief that we are entitled to a future of upward mobility.

The fact that the killer's first victims were women, including his own wife, the breadwinner for the family, may indeed have been random, and it might never have factored into his "irrational" thinking that in 1966 women in America were moving more purposefully toward equality with men. It is interesting to note, however, as we'll see in later chapters, that he is far from the only mass public shooter who seemed to have targeted women.

There's little doubt that the killer expected to become famous, just as many killers after him would. His writings demonstrate that expectation. He was writing for an audience. Nor is it in dispute that many of the killers who came after him demanded fame, videoing themselves in preparation or writing overwrought manifestos, all with an eye toward making a big splash in the media and cementing their awful legacies. The killer who murdered thirty-two people at Virginia Tech in 2007, for instance, even mailed his press kit to NBC News before he set off to commit mass murder.

But was it just a fluke of history that the massacre at the Tower, the first but far from the last mass shooting covered live coast to coast, occurred just thirty-four months after Americans watched Jack Ruby gun down Lee Harvey Oswald, making us all witnesses to a homicide and turning both murderers into near-mythic creatures?

And what are we to make of the fact that the deadliest mass public shootings in history have all occurred since 2007? That the controversial 1994 assault weapons ban expired at precisely the moment that America's poorly kept promise of upward mobility for everyone began to recede in the Great Recession, fanning a smoldering sense of grievance among many in America?

Is it significant that these events coincided with the explosive spread of the Internet, putting both a virtual support community and instant undeserved celebrity at the fingertips of any would-be killer with a keyboard and a grudge?

That is not to say that some among these killers did not endure some form of victimization or childhood trauma. Indeed, about a third (31 percent) of mass shooters had experienced severe childhood trauma, and that number was far higher among school shooters. Some 68 percent of the latter had reportedly experienced childhood trauma, according to the Violence Project Database of Mass Shootings in the United States, 1966–2019.[21] And there is no question that trauma, as we'll see later in this book, is and should be among those factors considered when assessing the various experiences and impulses that combine to turn a person into a mass shooter.

But it's also true, says Kelly, that what many of these killers claim as victimhood is sometimes little more than their own experience of the disappointments and failures common to most people. And often, in their grandiosity and narcissism, they concoct overwrought and overarching societal excuses for their shortcomings. They cast themselves as the heroes of their own neurotic sagas, often identifying a cause outside themselves for those personal failures and disappointments and portraying their murderous impulses against the innocent as acts of well-deserved revenge.

Take the twenty-two-year-old killer from Isla Vista, California, who in 2014 shot and stabbed six people to death—three of them women, all of them students at UC Santa Barbara—and wounded fourteen others before shooting himself in the head in what he ostentatiously called a day of "Retribution." Just before the murders, the killer, the troubled, withdrawn son of a sometime Hollywood filmmaker and his actress wife, posted a video on YouTube and scrawled a rambling and self-aggrandizing 144-page manifesto in which he carefully catalogued every perceived insult he had experienced in his life. He expressed hatred of minorities, though he was half-Asian himself, and of women and men who unlike himself were sexually active. He likened himself to a "god" and lamented that since puberty he had never succeeded in romantic endeavors with women, who for him were clearly objects to be possessed and dominated. He saw his status as an "incel"—an involuntary celibate—not as a self-caused problem but rather as the result of a cultural cabal of feminists and liberals and entitled popular young men who had all conspired to cheat him out of his God-given right to sow his seed as he saw fit, regardless of what any potential partner might want. Women existed, in his mind, to serve creatures like him, and sexually active men were taking what was rightfully his. So he set out to avenge himself on them. In his YouTube video, he boiled it all down to this:

> You forced me to suffer all my life; now I will make you all suffer. I waited a long time for this. I'll give you exactly what you deserve, all of you. All you girls who rejected

me, looked down upon me, you know, treated me like scum while you gave yourselves to other men. And all of you men for living a better life than me, all of you sexually active men. I hate you. I hate all of you. I can't wait to give you exactly what you deserve, annihilation.[22]

Again and again, over the past half century, we've seen cases where narcissistic killers lay the responsibility for their actions not on themselves but on some Other: women, minorities, the gay community, immigrants, and sometimes those of their own class and culture more successful at any endeavor than they might be. They take the prejudices that still permeate modern American culture and distill them into an even more toxic potion that they then use to absolve themselves and justify murder. And then they call themselves the victims.

In about 14 percent of the mass shootings that have been committed since 1966 in America, according to the Violence Project database, that sense of victimhood is expressed through a racial prism, targeting people because of their skin color. In just under 10 percent of the cases (9.4 percent), the killers appear to be motivated by misogyny, the study found, and in another 6.5 percent, the slayings are linked to religious bias.[23]

Make no mistake. Killers who specifically target women hate and resent women. Racist mass killers are racists. And they find solace in virtual communities of racists. Anti-Semitic murderers are anti-Semites, and they find common cause with other anti-Semites in the digital universe. But first and foremost, they are killers, people who see themselves as both avengers and victims and who often seek validation for their murderous fantasies. It's no surprise that they would seek it among people in movements—especially white supremacist and anti-women and antiminority groups—that thrive on a false sense of victimhood.

"There are people who experience trauma that involves the real life and death of loved ones, and other personal circumstances—being born into extreme poverty, something like that. We shouldn't discount those things," Kelly says. "But I think the culture of victimhood that's . . . circulating on the Internet is . . . as if the experience of the general frailty of being human and the vulnerability we all have to trauma is . . . being confused for the systematic victimization and oppression of an entire class of people."

Many factors that feed on each other have created the conditions in which this epidemic of gun violence rages in America and have created the environment in which these killers are nurtured. Some are broadly cultural. Some are deeply personal. Some can be measured by caliber. And some are difficult to measure at all.

We want so desperately to find a single silver bullet to explain away all the deadly lead ones that have been fired since. A fully formed and purely political motive. Violence on screen. A school prayer not said. A tumor.

It may be none of those things. Or it may be a bit of all of them.

It may be that we live in a heavily armed society in which many of us are afflicted to some degree by the same disease that infects these murderers, though in most of us the malignancy never becomes lethal.

For most of us the fever never burns as hot as it does for mass public shooters. But perhaps because it afflicts so many of us, because so many of us show the symptoms, it's difficult if not impossible to recognize that malignancy before it turns lethal in the most murderous among us. Until it's too late.

If it was true in 1966 that the killer in the Tower was just like us, only more so, perhaps it's truer still today.

CHAPTER 2

Deliver Us from Evil

HIS WIFE KNEW better than to ask. And he was grateful for that. He knew she'd seen the newscasts all day long, on an endless loop—the same footage from the helicopters and the same telephoto shots from the ground; too far away, too grainy to make out the awful details. But close enough to capture the horror.

The sturdy and modest one-room Amish schoolhouse, backed by a cloudless sky on a glorious 70-degree October day in Lancaster County, Pennsylvania, had been turned into a charnel house. At least the media had enough restraint not to show the bodies of the slain, innocent beyond words: eight young Amish schoolgirls, ranging in age from seven to thirteen, shot at point-blank range, five of their bodies laid out in a line like cornhusk dolls inside the white picket fence their fathers had built around the school building.

She knew the instant he called that he'd been in the middle of it. "You're gonna see some stuff all over the news," he warned her. "I'm okay. I don't know what time I'm gonna be home."

She'd been married long enough to this flinty state trooper from Philly to know that was all she was going to get out of him, for now. She'd often teased him about having become jaded in his years on the force. But she knew better. Sooner or later, in his own terse way, he'd tell her what happened that day: how he and nine of his men had faced off against this murderer with a personal grudge against God, who was going to exact his revenge by killing as many of His most innocent children—all of them girls—as he could.

He'd tell her how he and his men formed a perimeter around the place, assuming—just as the cops at Columbine High School had seven years earlier—that this had to be a hostage situation, because the alternative, that it was a coldly calculated mass murder designed in every detail to maximize its horror, was just too awful to imagine.

He'd tell her how wrong he was.

She'd learn, as all of us would, that the killer had planned and prepared for more than just murder. In addition to the shotgun, the rifle, and the semiautomatic pistol he had brought with him to the school that day, in addition to the six hundred rounds of ammunition and the change of clothes he had collected in the days and weeks before the murders (just as the ex-Marine in Austin had a generation earlier), he'd also brought plastic ties to restrain the children and personal lubricants, evidence that he also plotted to defile them before he killed them, to heighten the affront to the Almighty. The fast arrival of the cops on the scene had, at least, spared the children that.

Eventually, he'd tell her how he and his men had forced their way through the defenses the killer had erected—how the killer had used the meticulous craftsmanship of the Amish carpenters to buy himself time. He'd tell her how the killer had shuttered the windows, how he had culled the children he planned to kill, freeing the boys and holding the girls, and how their teacher, not much more than a girl herself, had managed to escape, finding her way to a nearby farmhouse with a telephone and summoning help.

He'd tell her about the standoff, about the exchange of fire with the killer, revealing how the murderer had fired a blast from his shotgun directly at him and how he had been saved only by the cover provided by the killer's pickup truck, parked at the doors of the schoolhouse as a barricade. He'd tell her about watching as the murderer blew his own brains out and about the hellish darkness and the stench of gun smoke, when they finally made it inside. He'd tell her how he and his men stepped over the killer's body, toward the blackboard at the head of the room where the girls had been forced to lie in a neat row before the gunman shot them. He'd tell her how he and his men each grabbed a girl and carried them outside into that blindingly bright Pennsylvania afternoon.

And he'd tell her about the hardest order he'd ever had to give, how one of his troopers had carried out a girl, clearly beyond help but still with a faint pulse. "Stay with her," he ordered the trooper. So she wouldn't die alone.

He'd remember how he looked up from the dying girl's body, across the trimmed lawn, to the picket fence where the girl's anguished parents stood watching their child die. "Stay there!" he barked. Though he'd never use the word—it's a civilian word, too emotional—it would haunt him forever that they obeyed. No matter how much they wanted to rush to their dying daughter's side, they'd obeyed. He never would have obeyed such an order himself. "If it's my daughter with a gunshot wound, nobody's telling me to stay back," he thought. But "the Amish are very obedient people. You tell them to stay back, and they stay back." And he'd tell her someday how those same grieving parents had come up to him afterward and thanked him for having someone stay with her, for making sure that "she wasn't alone for her last moments."

He and his men had been prepared that day to "give a life, save a life, or take a life." That was their mantra and their shield, drilled into them since their days at the state police academy. What he wasn't prepared to do was talk about it. Not yet.

"I don't know when I'll be home," he told his wife.

And because she was a cop's wife, she knew that was all he was going to say.

And she gave him the only response a cop's wife ever could under those circumstances.

"OK."

She didn't say much more when he came home after midnight. She just watched as he climbed the stairs to his five-year-old daughter's bedroom, gently scooped the sleeping child into his arms, carried her to a chair, and rocked with her in silence for forty-five minutes. Because she knew as well as he did that there was nothing else he could do.

That very night, the fathers and the brothers of some of the slain also did the only thing they could possibly do in the face of such a horror. They made a pilgrimage. Not to the schoolhouse, the scene of the massacre, but to the murderer's home. There, they consoled the killer's widow, and themselves. They allowed that "evil" had been done that day. But, they told the widow and her father, they were there to offer forgiveness.

In the days immediately after the massacre, those words would give comfort to some people. But they'd also be appropriated by others—weaponized and used as a cudgel to impose and enforce the deep and deafening silence between gunshots. That act of seeming selflessness and grace would become the story. The only story. It would all but drown out entirely any discussion about the malignancy in the psyche of the killer, and it would be wielded to shut down debates about guns or mental health, closing off any examination of the signs and portents that were missed or misread.

With the wounds of the terrorist attack on 9/11 still in their minds, with the body count still rising in our wars to avenge it, others—primarily those on the left side of the culture war—would appropriate the notion of Amish forgiveness to change the subject altogether, making it about American militarism abroad rather than about mass murder—and the murder of girls in particular—at home. For example, Sister Joan Chittister, a nun and noted author, writing in the *National Catholic Reporter* on October 9, 2006—four days after the massacre—would use the grace the Amish showed that evening to shame us for our wars abroad.

"It was not the murders, not the violence, that shocked us," she writes.

It was the forgiveness that followed it for which we were not prepared. It was the lack of recrimination, the dearth of vindictiveness that left us amazed. Baffled. Confounded.

It was the Christianity we all profess but which they practiced that left us stunned. Never had we seen such a thing.

Here they were, those whom our Christian ancestors called "heretics," who were modeling Christianity for all the world to see. The whole lot of them. The entire community of them. Thousands of them at one time.

The real problem with the whole situation is that down deep we know that we had the chance to do the same. After the fall of the Twin Towers we had the sympathy, the concern, the support of the entire world.

You can't help but wonder when you see something like this, what the world would be like today, if instead of using the fall of the Twin Towers as an excuse to invade a nation, we had simply gone to every Muslim country on earth and said, "Don't be afraid. We won't hurt you. We know that this is coming from only a fringe of society, and we ask your help in saving others from this same kind of violence."[1]

Even months and years after the massacre at West Nickel Mines, it would be the rare voice that would remind us that this was not an attack on the Amish alone; it was an attack on all of us.

The story we told ourselves would be a story of a man with guns and murder on his mind, and more. It would be a story framed by other men with guns who heroically confronted him, and the story would reach its climax when still more men granted forgiveness for the crime. A crime against girls.

It would be the lonely quiet voice in the cave that would remind us that this was not the first attack on females—studies have shown that girls are often the first to suffer in these atrocities. As poet and author Julia Kasdorf writes in the academic journal *CrossCurrents*, in an article published nine months after the atrocity, "Perhaps the enthusiasm for 'Amish forgiveness' expresses an understandable but irresponsible longing for graceful narrative closure to a horrible scene we would rather not examine, feel or understand—and the sexual and gendered nature of the attack is one aspect of the story's meaning that gets lost in the rush to forgive."[2]

But such voices had a hard time being heard over the siren call of forgiveness.

In effect, the culture at large seized on the granting

of absolution to one man's family and stole it: either to damn us for different sins or to grant absolution to us all. That phrase—"Amish forgiveness"—would be repeated in news stories across the globe more than 2,400 times in just the first seven days following the killings, according to research done by author and Amish expert Donald Kraybill, a professor and senior fellow at the Young Center for Anabaptist and Pietist Studies at Pennsylvania's Elizabethtown College.[3]

What got lost in that rush to stretch Amish forgiveness so thin that it covers us all is the understanding that the concept of forgiveness does not mean to the Amish what it means to the rest of us. In the Anabaptist and Pietist tradition of the Amish and the Mennonites, forgiveness is *not* synonymous with absolution. That can only be granted by God.

And it is not a choice. It is a commandment, an obligation, a willingness to submit—without question—to the judgment of an inscrutable God, even when that God allows a murderer to execute little girls in their classroom. It is an obligation to accept whatever God permits—even if it's "evil."

Evil.

That word *does* mean the same thing to the Amish that it does to the rest of us.

It's a word we have used time and again to describe these atrocities. When a gunman opened fire on congregants at a Fort Worth, Texas, church in 1999, killing seven, then governor George W. Bush laid the blame on "a wave of evil" sweeping across this nation.[4] When Stephen Willeford, one of the heroes of the Sutherland Springs church massacre in 2017, called to the gunman inside the church, it wasn't a man he summoned to face him in the street. It was, he told me, the embodiment of pure evil. It's become so woven into the fabric of our discussions of these atrocities that it's not inconceivable that one of the Columbine killers was mocking us with the concept when he allegedly—and perhaps apocryphally—asked one young girl, "Do you believe in God?" before shooting her point-blank through a library table.

"Evil" is a convenient word, and it may even give solace, for it holds out the hope that someone's loved one died not in a random act of cruelty but as part of an epic struggle between the forces of good and evil—a struggle that will, they believe in perfect faith, conclude with the ultimate victory of good in the End Times.

The idea certainly gave solace to the family and friends of Cassie Bernall, a seventeen-year-old evangelical Christian and a junior at Columbine High School, who is still in many places remembered as the "martyr" who died standing up for her faith, even as she kneeled under a table, inches from a mass murderer's shotgun.[5]

The notion that evil can be conquered certainly gave solace to her mother, Missy, who, in perfect faith that the story was true, penned a book, *She Said Yes: The Unlikely Martyrdom of Cassie Bernall*, and it no doubt gave comfort to the thousands upon thousands who turned that book into a *New York Times* best seller.

It matters almost not at all that, as Dave Cullen (who wrote *Columbine*, the definitive treatise on that school shooting) later learned, another student, Valeen Schnurr, probably made that now famous, courageous declaration of faith. Or that she made it after she had already been wounded, or that she made it to the second killer, the less murderously manic of the pair, who had just weeks before asked the Four Questions himself at a family seder. It barely registers as a footnote in the synoptic canon we've come to take as gospel about these crimes that the killer, for whatever reason, spared her.[6]

In the chaos and confusion, a sixteen-year-old witness, it seems, had misattributed the now-famous quote to Cassie, and though I hesitate to call it a myth—it was more like an article of faith—a dogma was born that day that continues to color the way we think of that massacre and many of those that came after it. As we'll see throughout this book, a great many comforting myths are forged in gunfire. A great many pernicious ones are, too. Those myths die hard.

And the people all say, "Amen."

Because there can be great comfort in that notion of evil.

If indeed it is "evil" that drives these murderers, it follows that "thoughts and prayers" can exorcise the same evil, even if there must be martyrs along the way.

But there's also great peril in that definition of evil, says Rosa Eberly, an associate professor of rhetoric at Penn State (and before that at the University of Texas) who has spent decades in a kind of secular pilpul, trying to tease meaning out of the chapters and verses we use to define these atrocities.[7]

As Eberly writes in "Deliver Us from 'Evil'" (2003), "Claims about evil have dysfunctional consequences for deliberative discourse . . . because such claims conceal causes and obscure possible solutions." She asks, "How do claims about 'evil' help us work together to prevent school shootings and more general violence in our culture? How do they help us to prevent such things from happening again?" She concludes, "They do not. In fact, claims about 'evil' shut down deliberations."[8]

To the degree that we blame some force beyond human control for the deeds humans do, we grant ourselves absolution; we "forgive us our sins" of omission and commission.

Our more conventionally pious neighbors are, of course, not the only ones who cling to dogma. In the wake of these things, the secular chant incantations from their own books of charms, believing, in perfect faith, that because these killers have so often exhibited signs of mental illness, it follows that somehow, someday, we will find the right combination of scientific research and social, medical, and police protocols to identify them before they commit their crimes and either redeem them or restrain them. It's the same kind of fervent faith in science that led us to launch the Apollo missions to put a man on the moon less than three years after the Tower massacre. And it's the same kind of blind, hubristic faith in the boundless potential of science that contributed to the *Challenger* disaster, say some of those who are charged with analyzing the data around America's mass shooting epidemic.

To be sure, when you're looking at the narrow universe of mass public shooters, you find that the majority of them are afflicted with some kind of mental health problem. Researcher and criminologist Grant Duwe at the Minnesota Department of Corrections, who has spent his career warning his colleagues and the public about leaping to conclusions over the causes of mass public shootings, has found that as many as 59 percent of them had either been diagnosed with some kind of mental illness or had, in hindsight, shown signs of it.[9] *Mother Jones* magazine, which has compiled over the years one of the most comprehensive databases on mass public shootings, puts the number at 61 percent.[10]

There's no question that many of these killers are afflicted by mental health issues. But so are 46.6 million other Americans in any given year—one in five, according to the National Alliance on Mental Illness. That's a very big haystack to search. If you go looking, it's far more likely that you'll find a potential target of violent crime, the experts tell us. According to a 2005 study published in the *Journal of the American Medical Association*, people suffering from mental illness were up to twenty-three times more likely to be raped, robbed, or attacked than those not suffering from a diagnosed mental illness.[11]

Nor can it be assumed, even after the fact, that a

particular manifestation of mental illness led inexorably to a particular bloody conclusion.

Take the young murderer who wrapped himself—figuratively and at times literally—in the Confederate flag, sat down with a prayer group in Charleston, South Carolina, at the Emanuel AME Church (lovingly called Mother Emanuel for the role it has played in African American history), and then murdered nine of them—six women and three men—in cold blood.

Court documents released after a jury in federal court convicted him and sentenced him to death indicated that the murderer had been diagnosed in jail with a raft of psychological disorders: schizoid personality disorder, social anxiety disorder, a mixed substance abuse disorder, a history of depression, and a possible autism spectrum disorder.[12]

As many as 6.5 million Americans suffer from schizoid personality disorder, according to a study published in 2004 in the *Journal of Clinical Psychiatry*.[13] Some 15 million American adults suffer from some form of social anxiety disorder, the Anxiety and Depression Association of America tells us, and another 16.1 million struggle with major depression.[14] One in every sixty American children fits somewhere on the autism spectrum, and boys are four times more likely to be affected, according to the Centers for Disease Control.[15]

Millions of Americans grapple every day with the same demons the Charleston killer allegedly did. Only one of them sat down next to a group of worshippers, calmly read Bible verses with them, and then pulled out a Glock and shot them to death, declaring to anyone still alive to hear him, "I'm not crazy. I had to do this."

Nor is there any guarantee that, even if the stars are all perfectly aligned and we recognize a mental illness in a killer before a rampage, we have the will or the resources to respond appropriately.

It was no secret to anyone who knew him, for example, that the young Tucson man who murdered six people at a political event in the parking lot of a Safeway store and wounded thirteen more—including US Rep. Gabby Giffords—had long displayed odd, alarming, and at times even threatening behavior. His school, Pima Community College, found his behavior sufficiently disturbing that they asked him to leave, a decision that, in hindsight, may have fueled his violent impulses. Campus police had interviewed him even before he made a disturbing 2010 video in which he described PCC as "a genocide school," a video that in some ways mimicked similar tapes made by other killers, such as those at Columbine and Virginia Tech, to cite just two examples.

Court papers show that for over a year before the attack his parents watched his mental decline with mounting concern, and they even went so far as to try to restrict his access to both his shotgun and his car. He showed all the signs of schizophrenia, and yet, as my friend Tom Zoellner documents in his deeply researched account of the slayings, *A Safeway in Arizona*, there is no sign that any effort was made to force the young man into therapy and treatment. Not by his family, not by the school, not by the cops, even though, as Zoellner notes, under Arizona law any one of them could have tried. "An Arizona law passed in 2002 says that any 'responsible person'—a parent, a friend, a cop or even a total stranger—can start a legal process to get a sick person some treatment," Zoellner writes, adding that "most people in Arizona who reach the point of being brought before a judge do get committed."[16]

None of the people who could have brought him before a judge did so.

It's tempting to speculate about how things might have turned out differently at one particular Arizona parking lot on one particular Saturday afternoon in January 2011 if one obviously disturbed would-be killer had been forced into therapy.

Maybe it would have prevented that killing.

And then again, it might not have.

At the end of March 1966, four months before he climbed the Tower in Austin, the mass shooter voluntarily sat down with Maurice D. Heatly, a staff psychiatrist at the University of Texas, to discuss what he'd later describe in his self-referential writings as his "irrational thoughts."

According to his contemporaneous notes, the psychiatrist found "the muscular young man" to be "self-centered an[d] egocentric" and "oozing with hostility." The soon-to-be killer also admitted to beating his wife on more than one occasion and spoke at length about what can only be described as a dysfunctional relationship with his parents, who had recently separated.

But Heatly found no evidence of psychosis. He neither ordered nor recommended any urgent treatment, proposing instead that the killer "make an appointment for the same day next week." He added, helpfully, "Should he feel that he needs to talk to this therapist he can call at any time."[17]

He never called.

Certainly, psychiatry, psychology, our laws, and our understanding of the nature of violence have evolved in the five decades and counting since the "muscular young man" and the psychiatrist spoke. But they hadn't evolved enough by 2007 to stop the slayings at Virginia Tech.

There is no longer any question that the killer in what remains—for now—the deadliest school shooting in American history was mentally ill and was a danger to himself and others. But that diagnosis was not always so clear.

Yes, as early as middle school the young, isolated, and unusually uncommunicative Korean immigrant had been referred for therapy to deal with his anxiety and to help him break out of the wall of silence he had erected around himself.

It seems to have half worked.

By the time he reached eighth grade, he was still isolated. But he was no longer entirely uncommunicative. An art therapist who'd been working with him at the time suspected that the images he used—tunnels and caves, for instance—may have been signs of depression. He swore that he never considered harming himself or others, but all the same, his therapist drew up a contract with him in which he pledged to do no harm to anyone and to alert his parents or teachers if he began to think about mayhem.

A month after the Columbine massacre, he wrote "a disturbing paper in English class that drew quick reaction from his teacher. His written words expressed generalized thoughts of suicide and homicide, indicating that 'he wanted to repeat Columbine,'" according to the voluminous 2007 report on the slaying commissioned by then governor Tim Kaine.[18]

That behavior raised enough red flags that he was ultimately sent to see a psychiatrist at George Washington University, who concluded that the fifteen-year-old suffered from selective mutism and severe depression. He was temporarily prescribed paroxetine, a drug approved to treat depression, panic attacks, obsessive compulsive disorder, anxiety, and post-traumatic stress disorder. He remained on the drug for about a year and seemed to be improving.[19]

Virginia Tech knew none of this when he was admitted in 2003. No record of his treatment followed him to the university, though soon enough some of his teachers and school officials came to suspect that there was something deeply wrong with the young man. His teachers and his fellow students came to see him as a bitter loner jealously nursing a raft of resentments, especially, it seems, when it came to women and girls and those more affluent than him.

He now thought of himself as a writer, though his writing had become even more alarming, more lurid, more macabre, more violent. His increasingly worrisome behavior led to conflicts with his teachers and even a review by the university's Care Team, a unit designed to evaluate all aspects of student life. The Care Team did virtually nothing to respond, assuming that his teachers had all the tools they needed to deal with the young man, the Kaine Commission found. Teachers and counselors did indeed meet with him, repeatedly, but his behavior continued to become increasingly odd. He'd show up to sessions wearing dark glasses and be by turns coopera-tive, then belligerent. In his more cooperative moments, he'd follow through on the advice they gave him to contact mental health services at the school, and then he'd fail to show up for appointments.

There were signs of darkness outside the classroom as well. One of his suitemates remembered taking the sullen soon-to-be-killer to a party. He sat on the floor, stabbing the carpet over and over again with a folding knife all night long. It was the last time his suitemates invited him to a party.[20]

The crisis began to come to a head in December 2005 when he was accused of stalking a young woman, the same young woman whose carpet he'd stabbed repeatedly at the party. The campus police visited him. Though no charges were filed, they ordered him to steer clear of the young woman.

His encounter with the police seems to have shaken something in him. As soon as the cops left, he sent an email to his suitemate. "I might as well kill myself," he wrote.

His worried suitemate summoned police, and he was admitted to a nearby mental health facility, where a psychologist would determine that the man who would go on to commit mass murder was indeed mentally ill, but "does not present an imminent danger to [himself/others], and does not require involuntary hospitalization."[21]

That distinction—between requiring involuntary hospitalization under the law and allowing someone to submit to treatment of their own volition—may not seem like much of a difference. But as we'll see later, it may have been enough of a loophole to allow the killer to arm himself—perfectly legally—with a pair of semiautomatic pistols and kill thirty-two people, the first of whom was a woman.

After the mass murder at Virginia Tech, both the Commonwealth of Virginia and the federal government took the first halting and incomplete steps to tighten some gun and mental health reporting laws, bolstering, for example, the still-flawed National Instant Criminal Background Check System.

But if it's true, as gun rights activists so often tell us, that "guns don't kill people, people kill people," the handling of the Virginia Tech killer by his schools, by his counselors, by his psychiatrist and his psychologist, demonstrates graphically how much we still need to learn about how to manage our responses to people who might be likely to kill.

And what are we to make of potential killers who are not as obviously disturbed as the Virginia Tech killer, or the murderer in Charleston, or the gunman in the Safeway parking lot? What should we think, what guidance should we pray for to recognize in advance the 38 to 40 percent of these killers that Duwe and *Mother Jones* remind us do not so plainly bear the Mark of Would-Be Cain?

As Donald Kraybill points out in *Amish Grace*, cowritten with Steven M. Nolt and David L. Weaver-Zercher, the man who murdered the Amish schoolgirls had no known history of any mental illness. He'd never shown any especially aberrant behavior, never had a run-in with the law. Yes, the killer, who worked for his father-in-law driving a truck collecting milk from dairy farmers in Lancaster County, had a reputation for being ill-tempered. One of his clients went so far as to make sure his kids were not in the milk house during his appointed rounds because he was known to curse a blue streak while he was working.[22] But so do a lot of guys who spend their working hours sucking in the sickly sweet stench of souring milk by the hundred gallon and mucking around in mud and cow manure.

Some of those who knew the killer—or thought they did—would later tell investigators and reporters that a calm seemed to descend on the man in the days leading up to the slayings. In hindsight, some of them speculated that the calmness was a sign, a portent, a clue that he had crossed some awful threshold in his heart and in his mind, that he had devised his plan, committed himself to it, and now was just biding his time in a kind of homicidal serenity until the day of the murders. In hindsight. But beforehand? Would you have taken a warmer than usual "good morning" as a warning?

None of this is meant to suggest in any way that there is not an immense, urgent need to examine the flaws in our mental health system and the holes in our patchwork of state and federal laws that have allowed so many of these killers to slither through. Nor is it meant to criticize the tremendously valuable work being done on many levels, from the research units at the FBI to the guidance offices in schools across Texas and elsewhere, who try to coax out signs and portents, not from the cold descriptions of various mental illnesses contained in the *Diagnostic and Statistical Manual of Mental Disorders*, but from the study of the actual deeds of these killers.

As we'll see in chapter 6, that kind of risk-assessment approach may already have saved lives, and not just in places like New Middletown, Ohio, and Daytona Beach, Florida, where in 2019 risk assessment helped identify potential mass shooters in time to avert an attack. It reaches far beyond that by identifying those individuals who often model the same behaviors as mass public shooters but claim far fewer lives—sometimes members of their own families, sometimes their spouses, and often just themselves.

It's critical to remind ourselves that no matter what we think, no matter how hard we pray, there is no silver bullet to counter all the deadly lead ones.

It takes immense courage sometimes to see things as they are. Faith, in God or in science, can buttress that courage, but it cannot supplant it. That's the kind of courage it takes to sift through the clues left by many of these killers, clues that can take the most gentle and gracious things and turn them into poison.

In the hours after the mass shooting at Sandy Hook Elementary School, police descended on the killer's home, and there they found another crime scene. Before he killed twenty-six people, twenty of them elementary school children, he first murdered his mother in her bed. Analysts and researchers I've spoken to who saw the crime scene photos would remark how chillingly similar the photos were to those taken in another bedroom, half a century earlier, when the Tower killer murdered his own mother before beginning his rampage. As investigators fanned out through the house in Newtown, Connecticut, to the darkened, sparse bedroom where the killer had lived for months with little direct human contact apart from emails with his mother, they found clues to suggest that the similarities might not have been a coincidence. On the hard drive of his computer, they found an obsessively detailed list of all the mass public shooters who had come before him, in Jonesboro and Columbine and Virginia Tech. And yes, Austin.

They also found something else. Among a small collection of books, firearms manuals, the Federalist Papers, a book on the ways of the Samurai, and a handful more, one book stood out in glaring contrast to all the others.

It was *Amish Grace*.[23]

How odd it seems that a killer who was apparently obsessed with the most minute details of the atrocities that came before would pluck that one book out of the sea of books that have been written about these cases.

Kraybill, Nolt, and Weaver-Zercher's meditation on the Amish response to the murders at West Nickel Mines is hardly a pulpy true-crime book. It's not what those of us who have spent at least part of our careers detailing the sins we commit against each other derisively call "cop-porn."

It does not wallow in the gore of the killings, nor does it mythologize the killer. To the degree that it touches on the mass murder itself, it does so in a reserved, scholarly, and respectful way. It's a book that lives in the silence between the gunshots. Despite the dignified distance the authors try to keep, on every page you feel the bottomless grief of a community savagely attacked, the anguish of a deeply religious community that, despite its faith, was not spared the Tenth Plague. You feel the terrible weight borne by a community whose most innocent and vulnerable, its children, were slaughtered.

Why, of all the books ever written about such atrocities, did the killer choose to read a touching book about the inevitability of forgiveness in the face of horror?

Would answering that question give us any insight into the mind of this murderer, and would it perhaps tell us something crucial about the killers to come?

CHAPTER 3

To Kill
the Last
Killer

THERE WAS NOTHING in his demeanor to suggest that he was being anything less than forthright. He had answered every question precisely the way cops are trained to: be succinct, stick to the facts, and above all, report only what you observed. No matter how horrible.

The investigators asked again. "You never went into the classroom?"

"I took the perimeter," he said.

They knew there was no point in pressing him further. He wasn't lying, if lying means that one is consciously trying to deceive. At least he wasn't lying to *them*.

One or two of the other cops who had been there that day might have tried, intentionally or unintentionally, to mislead the investigators in ways that would not materially affect the outcome of the probe. Guys who might have hesitated a moment or two longer than they should have before going in may have omitted that detail in their reports, for instance. Almost every guy wants to imagine that he's a hero. Even heroes sometimes need to believe that they're more heroic than they are. You do enough after-action police reports, and you learn to expect a certain amount of self-image bias, and you learn to calibrate for it.

But this was different. This hard-bitten veteran cop had been one of the first officers on the scene. He had been part of one of the four-man teams that had burst into Sandy Hook Elementary School even before the full scope of the atrocity was fully understood, when all they knew was that at least one gunman with at least one semiautomatic rifle was loose in the school, and he was shooting children. His team hadn't hesitated. They rushed toward one of the two classrooms where most of the killings had taken place with one mission: *stop the killing, then stop the dying.*

They hadn't gotten there fast enough to do either. By the time they entered the classroom the massacre had already ended, and the killer had already blown his own brains out. The mass killing had lasted just eleven minutes from its bloody start to its bloody finish. They did not know that, of course, when they stormed into the building, passing the bodies of two slain adults and a wounded woman as they rushed down the hall and into the classrooms.

There are no words for what they saw that day. Children, twenty of them, not one of them older than seven, had been shot at close range by a killer armed with a Bushmaster rifle and hundreds of rounds of ammunition designed to inflict the most grotesque wounds to grown men on a battlefield somewhere.

And this cop had seen the worst of it. The three other

members of his team, all veteran cops themselves, men who had known and trained alongside this man for years, all swore that he was right there beside them, that he did exactly what they did and saw exactly what they saw.

"I took the perimeter," he insisted to the investigators.

That wasn't true. But he wasn't lying. At least not to them.

How do you measure a horror like the December 14, 2012, massacre at Sandy Hook?

Those who gaze at crystals will tell you with absolute conviction that the human soul weighs twenty-one grams, or so a physician and amateur researcher concluded in 1907 in a roundly debunked study.[1]

They're wrong, of course. It's far heavier than that. The weight of the souls of the twenty children and seven adults killed on December 14, 2012, was enough to bring most of this country to its knees, at least for a few days following the massacre. It was enough to bring a president to tears.

You can count bullets or bodies. You can measure blood spatters to the micron. But what is the measurement of horror?

Here's one metric. A veteran cop, a man who by temperament and training is supposed to be steeled to horror, is so overwhelmed by the atrocity he witnessed that his brain simply shuts down, refuses to record it, and replaces it instead with a false memory.

"I took the perimeter," he insists.

That's the measure of a horror that eclipses all the horrors that came before it.

And that, say researchers, analysts, and the cops who have studied the Sandy Hook massacre and other mass shootings, may have been precisely what the murderer had in mind as he plotted the atrocity in Newtown, Connecticut.

He was, by all accounts, a cypher, scrawny and

awkward, a loner by nature who had few friends in the real world—only two that investigators have been able to identify, and they were every bit as socially inept as he was. In the months leading up to the mass shooting at Sandy Hook Elementary School, he had cut off contact even with them, investigators say. In the photo that has circulated of him since the massacre, he has a wide-eyed, slack-jawed look, and, knowing what we now know about his deeds, we ascribe menace or madness to it. Of course we do. There is no silence on earth deeper than the silence between gunshots. It's only human nature that we try to fill it, stuffing it with all our suppositions and conjectures, half-truths and misconceptions.

But if you had happened to run into him in the days before the murders, on one of his few outings from the lair he had created for himself in the suburban house he shared with his divorced mother, if you had noticed him at all at the local movie complex where for hours upon hours he'd frantically wave his scrawny arms and flail his skinny legs trying to keep up with the ever-increasing beat of the electronic game *Dance Dance Revolution*, would you have seen a murderer, or just another goofy kid in a lobby full of them?

He must have been bullied, we tell ourselves, grasping for the catch-all explanation we've tried to apply to scores of such killers, from Columbine to Virginia Tech, though there's no clear evidence in any of those cases that it's true. *He must have nursed some festering grudge against the school*, we opine, despite the evidence that the days he spent there were, as Detective Daniel Jewiss, the lead investigator on the case for the Connecticut State Police, told me, "among the happiest days of his life."

He must have been mentally ill, we tell ourselves. *Somebody somewhere along the line must have dropped the ball, missed a red flag or two or a dozen, to let this killer loose on the rest of us.* Indeed, like millions of young Americans, mostly males, he had been diagnosed as fitting on the autism spectrum with a form of Asperger syndrome.[2] So had at least one of the children he killed. He also had an anxiety disorder and obsessive-compulsive disorder.

No one who has studied the case, least of all the Office of the Child Advocate of the State of Connecticut, which examined every detail of the young murderer's interactions with the mental health system from the time he was in preschool, disputes that more could have been done to address his mental health issues.

He had always been frail, physically and emotionally, and his mother would suggest to medical personnel that he suffered from a seizure disorder, though a full neurological workup was never done on him.

Before he was three, he had shown signs of developmental problems. He slept little and fitfully; there'd be bursts of manic energy, and then he'd retreat into a world of his own making and communicate very little. "He made up his own language," the Office of the Child Advocate report found.[3] An evaluation done on him when he still lived in New Hampshire found that he "fell well below expectations in social-personal development," especially when it came to language.[4] But his mother was always there to interpret for him. She was, and would remain, his doorway to the world outside, right up until the moment he took a .22-caliber Savage rifle, one of several firearms the self-described gun enthusiast bought to enjoy with her son, and shot her to death with it in her sleep before launching his attack on the school.

He was bright enough, and could at times be almost charming and funny, but, like many on the autism spectrum, he would recoil at the touch of another human being and once again retreat into his own world, speaking a language that no one except he, and to some degree his mother, could understand. He was given to temper tantrums—indeed he always would be. But in between these episodes, he functioned well enough that by the time he was five, the school district concluded that whatever disabilities he might have, they did "not interfere with educational abilities."

Nor did they serve as any kind of warning of what was to come.

As the panel report notes in big, bold letters, while the boy who became a killer's "developmental and educational history provides important insights into his life experience, none of [that history] *predicted* he would become a mass murderer."[5]

While the records are incomplete, it does appear that the same issues that affected the killer as a young child continued throughout his years in school. With one very notable exception.

In 1997, the family—the killer, his father, his mother, and his older brother—then still intact but starting to show signs of significant strain, left New Hampshire for Connecticut in search of what the killer's mother would later describe as a "fresh start."

For the family as a whole, it didn't work out. In letters and emails that surfaced after her death, the killer's mother complained of a sense of near abandonment. Though he did try to make time for the boys on weekends—there was even one memorable camping trip he took them on—her husband, she wrote, "was a workaholic" who would leave the house and his stay-at-home wife before the kids awoke. Most days he'd return long after they had gone to bed. "There were worse things than that," she confided to a close friend, though she did not elaborate.

It is, of course, painful for everyone involved when a marriage hits the rocks. It is also not uncommon. About 9 percent of the 947,328 people living in the killer's adopted home county of Fairfield are divorced, according to the 2010 federal census.

By 2002 the marriage was effectively over. The killer's father and mother permanently separated, though they didn't obtain a decree of divorce until seven years later.

Yet none of this seemed to disturb the future killer. To the degree that he acknowledged the separation at all, he shrugged it off, telling one counselor that he just figured that his "parents 'irritated' each other as much as they irritated him."[6] It's not at all clear that he felt his father's absence in any significant way. After all, he had only seen him on weekends before the separation, and that hadn't changed measurably after it.

On the contrary, after he was enrolled at Sandy Hook Elementary School, he seemed to almost thrive. Yes, he was still awkward and withdrawn, and yes, his mother still hovered over him. She was still his portal to the world outside himself, though the record suggests that she had issues of her own. By 1999 she was writing melodramatic missives to friends telling them of various illnesses she was combating, hinting darkly in one, for example, that she didn't think she "had much time left," though a thorough review of her medical records after her murder found nothing to substantiate her complaints of ill health. She claimed in her letters that she was "putting on a big brave face for [her] family." Maybe she was. In any case there's no indication that the future killer was aware at all of his mother's real or imagined illnesses, or if he was, that they bothered him at all.

Indeed, years later, one of his former classmates, not quite a friend but a cordial acquaintance, would remember him at the time as "a nice kid, a little withdrawn." He was, maybe, "a bit off," the former schoolmate recalled, but "he seemed to get along with everyone."

One year he invited the future killer to his birthday party, and there was nothing remarkable about his behavior, though he added, "The one thing I thought was odd was that [his] mother stayed for the entire party."[7]

His mother would later say that it was at Sandy Hook that the future killer for the first—and maybe only—time in his life seemed to "enjoy being a kid." He did typical kid stuff, playing with Legos and performing in the school play. He even played baseball for a couple of summers, though later he would tell a counselor that he only did those things because his mother made him do them.

By the time he hit the third grade, his teachers noted in an interim report that he made a "concerted effort to volunteer answers" in class. His written work was "neat and thoughtful." By the fourth grade he was no longer in special education classes.

Overall, as one teacher described the future mass murderer, he was "a good citizen."

Albeit one with a taste for the macabre. In fifth grade, for a school assignment, he and one of those few real-world friends, a boy who would later be diagnosed as mentally ill and hospitalized, crafted a comic book in a purple spiral binder. It was a lurid, violent, and grotesque fantasy. The Sandy Hook killer and his friend dubbed it "The Big Book of Granny"; it was the continuing saga of a murderous crone, and it was full of episodes of cannibalism, human taxidermy, and, yes, child murder.[8]

In hindsight, perhaps, the comic book was grotesque enough that it should have broken through the white noise of a culture steeped in violence. Mental health experts who contributed to the report of the Child Advocate's office described it as "extremely abhorrent." The report continued: "If it had been carefully reviewed by school staff, it would have suggested the need for a referral to a child psychiatrist." But they also noted—"strongly caution[ed]" are the words used—that neither "The Big Book of Granny" nor anything else they found in compiling the 114-page report "would predict that [he] was likely to commit mass murder, even if a better connection had been made between the writing of 'The Big Book of Granny' and a need for mental health evaluation and intervention."

Knowing what we know now, maybe it should have been seen as an indication of something more ominous than the usual childhood preoccupation with gore that goes back to the days when the Brothers Grimm first put quill to parchment. Maybe. But it's hard to spot a single red flag in a Black Forest full of them.

If there was any alarm, it was muted.

The two young scribes were proud enough of their grotesque comic book that there are reports that they tried to sell copies of it to their classmates for twenty-five cents a pop. It's not clear whether they found any buyers. It does appear, according to the report, that at least one school administrator broached the subject with the killer's mother. But there's no record of any other official response by the staff or the administration or his mother to the book or its sale.

It now appears that his time at Sandy Hook was the high point of his school career, a brief period when—with notable exceptions, like the crafting of "The Big Book of Granny"—he seemed more comfortable in the world outside himself than he had ever before or would again. By the time he was enrolled in the Reed Intermediate School, he began to withdraw again, refusing eye contact and keeping his distance from classmates. There is no indication that he was bullied or mocked during this period, not at school and not in his neighborhood. In social settings— on the school bus on the way home, for example—he'd retreat into his own world, closing his eyes and drowning out any real-world sound with his headphones. In other words, from the outside he looked like pretty much any other preteen boy, unless you happened to look closely at his hands, which he had rubbed raw from incessant washing, a sign, it would be suggested in hindsight, of his obsessive-compulsive tendencies.

By seventh grade—now at the Newtown Middle School—the old behaviors were aggressively reasserting themselves: his social anxiety and isolation, the lack of communication with others, the emotional instability and inability to process stress. In the third quarter of that year, he was abruptly withdrawn from Newtown Middle School and enrolled at a nearby parochial school.

He didn't fare much better there. And again, the fascination with the lurid, the violent, and the macabre would resurface. As one of his teachers, quoted in the report, recalled, "I remember giving creative writing assignments to students, instructing them to write a page or two on whatever they wanted to talk about. . . . [He] would write ten pages obsessing about battles, destruction and war."[9]

"I have known 7th grade boys to talk about things like this," she is quoted as saying. "But [his] level of violence was disturbing. I remember showing the writings to the principal at the time, [his] creative writing was so graphic that it could not be shared."

Yet that same year, prodded by his teacher to write a piece that did not include death or destruction, he crafted a poem that was, in her words, "beautiful"—so beautiful that his father, who had come to the school to hear his son read the poem aloud in class, cried when he heard it. We can only wonder what the boy who would become a mass murderer of children made of that. Did he understand that tenderness can sometimes bring a man to his knees just as surely as brutality can? And would he one day devise a way to weaponize it?

The killer withdrew from the parochial school at the end of the year. He took two things with him. One was his school uniform, which he would continue to wear long after he had left the school, keeping it as part of his rotation of outfits he would cycle through obsessively, sometimes changing several times a day. The other was an abiding disdain for organized religion, an antipathy that one psychiatrist later described as an obsession. A few years later, while he was completing high school at home, a therapist asked him an anodyne question: If you could have three wishes, what would they be? His answer, the therapist noted, was that "he would wish that whatever was granting the wishes would not exist."[10]

In September of the following school year, there was an incident in which the killer's mother again asserted herself as the doorway between the killer and the world outside himself. Sometimes, like at Sandy Hook, that door opened as wide as she could open it. Other times, it appears, she looked for ways to hold it shut. It's not clear exactly what precipitated an emergency room visit that September. The killer's mother would later say that she brought her son to Danbury Hospital that day for the sole purpose of getting a note to allow him to stay home from school indefinitely. She insisted that he'd be more comfortable there, less agitated. Protected.

The hospital's crisis team saw a frail, shaky, 5-foot-8-inch, 98-pound patient who was anxious and withdrawn. Hypervigilant and fearful, he withdrew from the slightest touch. They wrote up a diagnosis that once again mentioned Asperger syndrome and obsessive-compulsive disorder, both of which afflict millions of Americans, and they recommended that hospital staff do a full psychiatric workup on him with an eye toward creating a therapeutic regimen.

His mother resisted.

A compromise was reached. The hospital staff wrote a note excusing the future killer from school for three days, and the killer's mother promised that she'd bring him back to the ER if his behavior further deteriorated.[11]

He did, soon after, begin seeing a private local psychiatrist and spoke with him some twenty times, investigators found. Whatever he and the psychiatrist talked about is lost to history; any records that might have existed had been destroyed or discarded by the time investigators started looking for them after the shooting at Sandy Hook. Whatever it was they recorded, it was not particularly memorable. The psychiatrist told state police investigators in 2012 that he barely remembered the killer.

One of the few documents that did survive the de facto purge was a note from the psychiatrist recommending that the future killer should no longer be required to attend classes and should instead be schooled at home—homebound education, it's called.

There is no indication that the school district second-guessed the psychiatrist, no sign, as the Child Advocate's report says, that the district's experts "considered any potential detrimental effects of this home-bound placement for [him]." Nor does the record suggest any reason why they would have questioned the psychiatrist's judgment, though the report faults the district for not demanding—as required—a more fulsome written report on the case from him.

Within the four walls of his increasingly constricted homebound educational environment, the killer retreated ever deeper into a world of his own. A year after he first met with the local psychiatrist, at the urging of his estranged father he was taken to Yale, where another psychiatrist again ticked off the same behaviors, which now seemed to be becoming more profound. He warned that there was a serious danger of further deterioration if the killer was allowed to become further estranged from the real world.

"There is a significant risk . . . in creating, even with the best of intentions, a prosthetic environment which spares him having to encounter other students or to work to overcome his social difficulties. Having the emphasis on adapting the world to [him], rather than helping him to adapt to the world, is a recipe for him to be a home-bound recluse, unable to attend college or work productively into his twenties and thirties and beyond with [his] mother becoming increasingly isolated and burdened," the psychiatrist wrote.[12]

Nothing changed. Except him. Just as the psychiatrist warned, he became even more reclusive. Earlier in his life he had seemed to enjoy the company of his older brother, but now he began to withdraw even from him. As the next few years passed, it seemed as if he was trying to abdicate from the analog universe. He erected real and virtual barricades between his mother and himself as well, communicating with her primarily via email, even though they were in the same house. His room became a lair. He tacked up sheets over his windows to block the world outside from view and to keep himself always in a climate-controlled, artificially lit cocoon, rarely straying far from his computer. He probed the outer limits of that cyber world rather than dwell in ours. He became adept enough at navigating cyberspace that once, when he was in what passed for him as the ninth grade, he reportedly attracted the attention of federal authorities after trying to hack into a government website. Nothing ever came of the probe, and the next time federal agents showed up in his neighborhood, they'd be investigating a mass murder. By the time he hit the tenth grade, he had withdrawn from most of his cyber classes.

He would spend a great deal of time obsessing over a couple of video games—yes, the immensely popular *World of Warcraft* was one of them, a game played by over 5.5 million people the world over, many of them just as obsessively. But there is no indication that the game incited him to violence or made him any more efficient as a killer. Indeed, as crime scene investigators reconstructed the killer's movements during the shootings, they discovered that they could tell exactly when and where the killer had reloaded, because in virtually every case, they'd find a live, unfired round on the floor there. The Internet might teach you how to tape two extended-round magazines together, as he would do before heading off to Sandy Hook. But video games don't teach you the rudimentary skill of swapping out a magazine on a Bushmaster without accidentally ejecting a live round from the chamber, investigators observed. You only learn that in the real world, a world the killer rarely visited.

And he was just as obsessed with the slapstick, comic-book mayhem of the Mario Bros. games. To suggest that those games somehow fanned his murderous urges would be a stretch, as much of a stretch as it would be to suggest that the self-defeating antics of Yosemite Sam might have somehow inflamed the murderer in Austin half a century earlier. That's not to say that popular music and popular art in general don't play a role in our culture of violence. Popular culture has, if nothing else, celebrated bloodshed and aggrandized killers, from Kinky Friedman's ode to the Tower sniper to the hit song "I Don't Like Mondays," which defined for most Americans the 1979 schoolyard shooting by a teenage girl in San Diego. Regardless of the authors' stated intent, it's created a kind of mythic anti-hero out of these killers, as evidenced by the "lullaby" the band Weezer recorded in honor of the eighteen-year-old murderer who took a Chinese-made knockoff of an AK-47 and mowed down people at his Massachusetts college in 1992. It's turned mass murder into a kind of white noise that is so widespread in our culture we don't even know we hear it anymore. Go ahead, sing the refrain from the more recent and infectiously catchy hit song "Pumped Up Kicks," depicting the imagined thoughts of a school shooter. You know the words.

No one is suggesting that those songs, or even those games, turn people into monsters. *Super Mario Bros. 2* doesn't kill people. People kill people.

But in a culture shrouded in a dense, comfortable fog of normalized violence, it's hard to figure out which silhouette in the fog is carrying a rifle or a semiautomatic handgun with deadly intent.

And what are we to make of the Sandy Hook killer's favorite game, the one he played most obsessively, for hours on end? *Dance Dance Revolution* had no violent overtones at all. And it consumed him. He had a home version. On occasion he would drive to the local multiplex in the black Honda Civic his mother had bought him (hoping it would entice him to visit the world outside), and once there he would play an industrial-strength version of the game—often solo—until the theater emptied out and the staff would unplug it. Was that a symptom of his OCD, perhaps? Was it an indication that in addition to everything else, the skinny, awkward child killer might also have had anorexia—a disorder that often is associated with depression—as some mental health experts have speculated?

What we know without question is that by the time he was in his teens, the killer was tenuously tethered to the real world by a coil of cords secured to the wall by three-pronged plugs. One acquaintance told investigators developing a profile of him after the killings about how "weirded out" this loner had been when Hurricane Sandy barreled through the Northeast, knocking out power to the entire region for days on end. He bunkered down in his bedroom, refusing to leave, refusing even to go to a hotel where he might have had access to power, a pattern that he would later reprise in the days before the massacre, when his mother threatened to move them to far-away Washington State or maybe Maine for another "fresh start."

There was, of course, one concession to the world outside that the killer was willing to make, if a little reluctantly. He lived in a house full of firearms in a country awash in them. His mother, a country girl by blood and upbringing, had grown up around guns, hunting and target shooting in rural New Hampshire. Her love of the shooting sports continued into adulthood. It was precisely in deference to seemingly reasonable, law-abiding folks like her that the 1994 federal assault weapons ban grandfathered in weapons similar to the .223 Bushmaster that her son would use to commit mass murder, meaning that millions of them remain in circulation. She bought hers in 2010, of course, after the ban had expired. But she could just as easily have picked one up while the ban was in place.

Despite her stated concerns about her son's mental health, the record shows that she enthusiastically shared her love of guns with him. As author Matthew Lysiak reports in *Newtown*, he first wrapped his finger around a trigger when he was four years old under the careful supervision of his mother, and throughout his childhood she would continue to take him to the range, making certain to observe every safety precaution.[13] His preoccupation with firearms continued throughout his life. Though he would spend less time at the range with his mother as he got older, he would continue to haunt websites and chat groups dedicated to gun enthusiasts, where he'd hold forth about the hardware with a kind of knowledgeable confidence and ease that was apparent nowhere else in his life, certainly not in the real world.

Those experts who have studied mass murderers, like Adam Lankford at the University of Alabama and forensic psychologist J. Reid Meloy, suggest that there are certain weapons, not whole classes of weapons but specific weapons, that take on an almost totemic significance among would-be mass murderers—more because of their appearance than the way they function and, more importantly, because of their association with mass murders of the past. And among those who take a perverse delight in the accounts of these mass killers' deeds, certain weapons become, as Meloy puts it to me, "fetish" items. We'll take a closer look at that idea in chapter 4. Suffice it to say for now that the .223 Bushmaster that the killer's mother kept in the house with him seems to be one of those fetishized weapons.

There are far darker corners of the web than those devoted to gun enthusiasts, and during the same period that the killer was sinking deeper into his digital isolation, they were spreading across the hidden recesses of the Internet like toxic toadstools. Whatever your kink, whatever your obsession, whatever your sin, there was a place for it, or soon would be. All you had to do was fever-dream it into existence. If you knew which keys to tap, you could find a community of people championing pedophilia, for example. The killer knew which keys to tap. Though there's no evidence that he trafficked in child pornography per se, investigators would later determine that he was known to visit at least one website that celebrated those who would exploit and abuse children. He would later tell an online acquaintance that he hated pedophiles, that he felt "sorry" for their victims to the extent that he was capable of feeling empathy for anyone, but he allowed that a sexual relationship between a predatory adult and a vulnerable child could "be beneficial to both."[14] After the slayings investigators found on his computer a lengthy essay he had written on the subject, ostensibly as a writing sample for college admission, which was never submitted. "As with the 'Big Book of Granny,' it was obsessive in both length and tone, 34 pages long even though he stated that the 'requirement' was 500 words," the Child Advocate's Office report notes.

In the years after Columbine and Virginia Tech—and a movie theater in Aurora, Colorado, less than six months before the atrocity at Newtown—virtual fan pages sprang up celebrating the killers and documenting the minutest details of their crimes. The more aggressive of the two killers from Columbine, sneaky, manipulative, and cruel in real life, was hailed as a rock star in this sordid make-believe world of the Internet. His moody, depressive accomplice became the Quiet Beatle of mass murderers to a legion of unmoored fans.

The Sandy Hook killer plunged into this digital swamp with both feet. Even among those enthralled with mass murder, his obsessive focus seemed beyond the pale. As the virtual acquaintance told investigators, "He was the weirdest person online."[15]

He rigorously analyzed and annotated a growing online list of mass murderers and their deeds. He studied their videos, their online rantings, and their rambling, grandiose manifestos. They became a fixation for him. As Meloy has written, that's hardly an uncommon phenomenon among those who go on to commit mass public shootings. Indeed, it's one of the flashing warning signs that FBI analysts cite in their report on the preshooting behaviors of active shooters, though all too often it flashes in the darkest corners of the web where few can see it. And even when those outside of that underworld can see it, it rarely flashes brightly enough to spark a reaction. Long after the massacre at Sandy Hook, reports surfaced that the killer had made some vague threats in an online chat against Sandy Hook Elementary School. There was nothing specific, but one of the participants in the chat was concerned enough to report it to police. He reminded them that the guy who made the nebulous threat lived in a house full of guns. He was told that there was nothing the police could do about it. The guns, after all, were perfectly legal and belonged to the mother.

It may have been around that time—some four years before the massacre—that the killer drifted across the critical line between fixation and what Meloy calls identification. It's the moment when a killer goes beyond saying, "I love this stuff, I love these videos, I love the weapons," beyond twisted hero worship of killers past, and begins to imagine himself to be one of them, passing through that narrow portal that links "what I think about all the time to who I become."

If there's one thing that most of these killers, even the most socially awkward, have in common, it's their seemingly boundless self-regard. They're narcissistic and grandiose even when they're pitiful and small. Perhaps especially when they are. As psychologist Roger Friedman (brother of songwriter Kinky Friedman, who lionized the murderer in Austin) wrote in *Tower Sniper*, his book with Monte Akers and Nathan Akers, that killer, like most who followed him, had "a preoccupation with fantasies of power, [a] sense of omnipotence, and [an] intense desire for admiration."[16]

Power. Control. If you're looking for a silver bullet to explain all the .223-caliber ones that the killer fired at the children and the adults who confronted him in Newtown that day a week and a half before Christmas in 2012, you won't find one. All the official reports on the slayings agree on that. But experts who have studied these cases tell us that there are often precipitating moments, events (or threatened events) that spark rage or murderous resentment and become the nucleus around which all the various other resentments and dark impulses and obsessions gather.

It seems likely, most of the official reports on the Sandy Hook massacre concur, that the decision by the killer's mother to consider a move to Maine or Washington State for another fresh start may have been one of those. It's odd. Why would he have cared? Why would it matter to an isolated young man who lived almost entirely in a virtual electronic cave what was outside that cave? Daniel Jewiss, the lead investigator for the state police, has a theory. He believes that the killer, who days earlier had fiercely refused to allow his mother to put up a Christmas tree, saw the potential move as a threat to his power, his need to control every detail of his life.

That of course does not explain murder on a massive scale, nor does it explain why he chose that peaceful, joyous place or why he targeted innocent children.

However, another trait that's been found to be common among mass public shooters might explain the Sandy Hook killer's choice of victims. As Meloy has noted, as these grandiose and self-obsessed killers compare themselves to their murderous role models, they often eventually find themselves competing with them. Among their hoard of resentments they add a new one, often against the very murderers that inspired them. They tell themselves that they can do better. Or worse. Far worse. "Not only do they want to imitate the guy, but they feel some envy because he had as many victims as he did, and in order to diminish their envy, they want to have more victims," Meloy says. As they imagine the carnage they will commit, as they plan for it and gird for it, they often throw one or two extra bodies on the top of the bloody bier: the bodies of the killer or killers who came before them. To put it simply, they often want to kill the last killer.

There is one piece of evidence collected from the killer's home that seems to point to that murderously competitive impulse in him. It's the book *Amish Grace*.

We'll never know conclusively why the killer had that book. He killed himself rather than submit to the power and control of the police who raced into Sandy Hook Elementary School to try to stop him.

But the analysts, experts, and investigators I have spoken with all concur that it is highly unlikely that the Sandy Hook killer saw that book as a tender, respectful, and mournful meditation on the grief of a community savaged by unspeakable violence against its most innocent children, but rather as a benchmark, a goal to be coldly met and cruelly surpassed. If the killer at West Nickel Mines could inflict such pain by murdering six girls and wounding five more, then the crushing weight of the deaths of twenty innocent children would be so much worse. It could bring a country to its knees, a president to tears, and it could erase the memory of a hardened, veteran cop. That would become the horror against which all others were measured. For a while.

It may not have been a desire for fame—or infamy— per se that led the Sandy Hook killer to glean what he could from *Amish Grace,* but rather a dark desire to commit an even more devastating atrocity. As Kraybill, one of the book's authors, put it to me in an email, he may have studied the book with the sole intent of "learning how to maximize the violence he could execute on young innocent kids."

It's a fool's errand to ascribe reason or logic to the actions of a mass killer, if by those words you mean the kind of logic and rational thought that governs most of us in our daily lives. There is nothing rational in the mass murder of schoolchildren or the members of a minyan or moviegoers at a cinema or students on a grassy mall. But that doesn't mean that there is not a kind of logic or cold rational calculation apparent in the minds of these mass killers. As Lavergne, the chronicler of the Austin Tower shooter, notes, every step that killer took in the days leading up to the massacre was carefully considered, targeted, intended to mask his actions right up until the moment he unsheathed his rifle to murder strangers with military precision—all, as Lavergne says, in service to himself. And in the decades since, scores of others have followed carefully in his footsteps, in many cases adding their own foul flourishes to them. And then other killers study them in search of inspiration.

Indeed, in the virtual shadows where these murderers often seem to school, in that dark place deep in the

Internet where the pop art paeans to violence that we think harmless are distilled down into a lethal elixir, these killers are often celebrated precisely because they so coldly and rationally killed according to the logic of that place. It's true that few, very few, of those who haunt these dark places will go on to become mass public shooters, or any kind of killer for that matter. Most just cower in the dark. To the degree that they act at all on their fantasies, they do it with vague, empty threats or hollow claims of responsibility for the criminal deeds of others, the experts tell us. In the hours and days after Sandy Hook, for example, as is the case after most similar mass killings, investigators were deluged with emails and text messages, false confessions, and warnings of future attacks to come, some targeting the parents of those children who had just been slain. Investigators had to spend precious resources tracking down every one of them, just in case one of them turned out to be real. Nothing ever came of them.

But for those who will kill, there is, just below our free market of ideas, a bizarre and twisted bazaar where would-be killers can model the trappings of murder worn by murderers before them like props and costumes in a play. This semiautomatic rifle. That black trench coat. Whole identities, patterns of behavior, off-the-rack justifications—social, political, personal—they can use to decorate their murderous impulses and make themselves seem more grandiose than they are, those are all waiting to be plucked.

Many years ago, while struggling with some demons of my own—they were, as the late poet and songwriter Leonard Cohen might have it, "middle class and tame"—I had occasion to meet with a psychotherapist, well regarded within a particular community of people, at his office on Manhattan's Upper West Side.

He had a bookshelf that stretched the length of the

wall behind his desk, but there were just three books on it. One was the Bible, the American Standard Version. The next was Freud's *Civilization and Its Discontents*. The third was the collected works of William Shakespeare.

"Everything you need to know to understand human nature is in those three books," he told me. At the time I thought it pompous, and that, I thought, was a charitable assessment.

"'Tis not alone my inky cloak, good mother, Nor customary suit of solemn black," a disturbed Hamlet chides his mother in the second scene of the eponymous play. "These indeed 'seem,' for they are actions that a man might play." By the end of the play, Hamlet has littered the stage with the bodies of five people he's murdered (including Rosencrantz and Guildenstern, his chums from school) and two more—the love of his life and his mother—whose deaths he caused. That's murder enough to qualify as a mass public slaying, as we define the term today.

I might have been wrong. That shrink all those many years ago might have been onto something.

CHAPTER 4

"'Tis Not Alone My Inky Cloak"

HE HAD NOTHING to fear. And he acted as if he knew it. As if he was sure that no one was likely to confront him, and even if someone tried, it would be futile. He was ready, and no one was going to have the power to stop him. He was sure of it. It'd be like blasting away at a flock of magpies dozing on a wire. There'd be dozens of people in that building on this beautiful early afternoon on one of the last few days of antipodean summer, on their knees, huddled together, murmuring prayers in a foreign tongue. So many targets he wouldn't even have to aim. But not one of them was ever going to shoot back. He was certain of that. Even if one of them had been armed—and none of them were—he'd have the element of surprise and enough firepower to drop them by the dozens before they had time to look up from their prayer mats. He'd be as safe in there as he was in the stark monk's cell of an unfurnished half-duplex that he called home.

And he knew it.

You could tell that by the easy way his right hand—in those fingerless gloves that are so often a part of the costume—skimmed around the edge of the steering wheel of his aging, car-lot Subaru. There was no tension in his hand as he drove, confidently, but carefully, down the streets of Christchurch, New Zealand. He didn't speed. He obeyed every traffic signal. Wouldn't want a ticket. He even pulled over for a moment—as any responsible motorist would—before turning his camera around to take a selfie. He struck a pose, mixing just the right measures of Mad Max menace and faux military bearing, as if he'd practiced it in the mirror. It's just the sort of thing that a narcissistic, unemployed, friendless gym rat would do, second nature for someone who spent hours almost every day obsessively humping four-hundred-pound weights to flog his body into something more than it really was. And then, taking care to signal, he eased back into the light Friday afternoon traffic.

He had been humming along to the cheery strains of an up-tempo folk song from Serbia, first recorded in 1993. It's not at all clear that he understood a word of the language, but he certainly understood the gist of the song. It was a sickly sweet tribute to Serbian strongman and convicted war criminal Radovan Karadzic, a paean to ethnic cleansing and genocidal mass murder accompanied by the merry trilling of a concertina. "Beware the Ustasha and the Turk," the song goes.

He wouldn't be the first to appropriate the mien of the ultranationalist Serbs to cloak his murderous urges.

Some five years earlier, a scrawny young man from Pennsylvania had proudly posed for a picture sporting the combat uniform of the Drina Wolves, a unit of the

Serbian Army that massacred 7,500 Bosnian men and boys in Srebrenica in 1995.[1] Not long after the photo was taken, that imaginary soldier skulked into the woods across the road from a remote state police substation and under cover of darkness opened fire, gunning down two troopers at shift change, killing one and critically wounding the other. Neither one of them was an Ustasha or a Turk. And three years before that, a thirty-two-year-old Internet troll had also wrapped himself in the bloody flag of Serb nationalism, and he still fancied himself some kind of "knight" when he was convicted of murdering seventy-seven people—most of them children, and most of them looking much like him—in a bombing and a sneak attack on an island camp in Norway. In a pretentious, rambling, self-referential 1,500-page manifesto, that killer uses the word "Serb" 341 times. It was eclipsed only by his use of the words "America" or the "United States"—in case there's any question about his other source of inspiration—which appear in one form or another 726 times, by my own counting.

That killer in Norway had become a hero to the young man in Christchurch. He would even claim he had spoken to that killer. And before he climbed into his rattletrap Subaru that afternoon, the aspiring killer in Christchurch had mailed his own seventy-four-page imitation of that manifesto to, among others, the prime minister of New Zealand. It was shot through with sarcasm and adolescent asides. It railed against indolent immigrants from elsewhere, though the aspiring killer in the Subaru was himself an immigrant from Australia who'd quit his job back home as a personal trainer and squandered the small inheritance his father left him after his suicide on a jaunt through Eastern Europe, among other places. In his imitation screed he tries to figuratively dress himself in the grandiose armor of mythic characters of the ancient past, leaders who fought against invaders from Turkey hundreds of years ago and whose exploits have been exploited ever since by tiny men to justify great atrocities against Muslims in that corner of Europe, in places like Srebrenica. It doesn't fit this killer well. It doesn't fit any of them well. They all look small and ridiculous.

The song was over by the time he eased his hatchback into the parking lot of the Al Noor Mosque. Now his tinny speakers struggled to hold a bravely chipper martial air more fitting to his Scottish, Irish, and English ancestry: a fife-and-drum song, "The British Grenadiers," a toy soldier of a tune that conjures gauzy images of lost empires for those who indulge themselves in such nostalgic fantasies.

The lot was crowded, but he quickly found a space, and of course, even though the spot was perfectly flat, he remembered to engage the emergency brake.

One can't be too careful.

There was no urgency, no sense of alarm as he casually wrapped his hand around the receiver of a black semiautomatic rifle he had kept on the passenger seat in plain view. It was one of those weapons that Adam Lankford tells us are so often fetishized by these killers, engineered to kill efficiently and designed and marketed to appeal to some soldier-of-fortune fantasy.

Of course it was.

The killer had decorated it, if you can call it that, with white supremacist symbols and the dates of great battles between the West and Islam more than half a millennium ago. In sloppy white paint he had scrawled the names of those ancient generals in that fight, along with the name of a more recent victim of a terrorist attack in Stockholm. It was as if he was shamelessly pilfering her pain and pirating their exploits for his own self-aggrandizement.

He eased out of the driver's seat and ambled to the back of the car. With his free hand he opened the hatch to expose, again in plain sight, two crudely fashioned improvised explosive devices, another semiautomatic rifle (similar in many respects to the one already in his hand), and a shotgun, also black and also covered with slogans scrawled in a childish hand in white paint. He chose the shotgun and sauntered off at a steady, but not in any way frantic, pace toward the front door of the mosque.

He didn't even bother to close the hatchback.

He didn't need to.

He had nothing to fear. And he knew it.

What followed over the next six minutes and thirty-nine seconds was a wholesale atrocity as horrible as any ever committed, anywhere; as vicious as the mass murder of children at West Nickel Mines and Sandy Hook, as murderously theatrical as the massacre of theater goers in Aurora, Colorado, by a killer who had adopted the visage of a cartoon villain.

We know every heartbeat of this part of the mass murder because in an act of supreme narcissism, the kind of narcissism at the heart of many mass shooters, the killer had live-streamed every second of it from the moment he first climbed into his Subaru.

The killing began when he was greeted at the door by a young worshipper who apparently didn't recognize the menace in the costume the intruder was wearing—the black tunic, the off-the-rack tactical vest—or who didn't see the garishly decorated killing machines in his hands, one of them fitted with a strobe light to blind and disorient the worshippers.

The young man welcomed the stranger, calling him "brother."

The killer murdered him where he stood.

It ended—or this part of the attack did, anyway—minutes later as he sauntered back to his car, past a young woman who, wounded, made it as far as the street. "Help me!" she cried as she lay facedown in the gutter.

"Help me!" He stepped to the curb and fatally shot her. In the back.

In between, while firing at up to three rounds per second, he killed forty-two innocent, unarmed people, most of them as they huddled together in corners of the mosque.

At one point during the attack, a young man, a head shorter and a stone lighter than the killer, jostled him. Perhaps, as the young man's family later said, he was indeed making a heroic attempt to grab the murderer's gun. Or maybe it was an accident. The video evidence is unclear. In any case, the young man bumped into him with no more force than might be expended by a retiree who elbows you while reaching for the second-to-last Christmas turkey in the frozen food section of Pak'nSave. It is clear that the killer was certain that he had nothing to fear.

The killer shot the young man from an arm's length away. The young man died soon afterward. For the remaining minutes he spent inside the mosque, the killer faced no other resistance, and he seemed to revel in that, to bask in it.

After shooting the worshippers—most were killed or wounded within the first two minutes of the massacre—he returned again and again to the same two piles of bodies, firing into them as fast as he could squeeze the trigger, not because he needed to fire quickly but simply because he could.

He was so unhurried that during the shooting he clumsily dropped an extended magazine and had the time to pick it up. A few moments later, he took a breather, strolled back to his car, retrieved his other rifle, and jogged back toward the mosque. Before going in, he stepped to an alley and fired a couple of rounds.

Maybe he saw a figure at the far end of the alley. Maybe not. But he exalted in the moment. "You're not going to get the bird today, boys," he said gleefully.

He then sauntered back into the mosque, stepping over the dead man by the door and two more he'd left dead nearby, then into the sanctuary where once again he senselessly fired round after round at those he had already shot.

And when he was finally finished with this part of the attack, he returned to his car—pausing briefly for one more murder along the way—and headed off to another mosque a few miles away where, though locked outside, he would kill nine more people before one unarmed man would unambiguously confront him and then pick up the empty shotgun the killer had dropped. The murderer—who finally did think he had something to fear—would turn tail and run. Police captured him a short time later. Needless to say, he didn't resist.

But several minutes before that, after the attack at Al Noor and en route to continue the massacre at the Linwood Islamic Center, the grotesque costume the killer wore fell away. He might try to sell his viewers—and perhaps even try to sell himself—on the notion that there was some political or cultural motive that somehow perversely accounted for what he had done. But the transparent mask of other people's ancient exploits and recent tragedies slipped. And the man behind them was naked for all the world to see.

As he stepped into his car, no cheery Old Empire military airs played, no rolling drums or brave fifes, no ethnic-cleansing drinking songs from somebody else's genocidal war. No. He was blaring "Fire" by the Crazy World of Arthur Brown, a hackneyed old hit that has whipped acned, hormone-poisoned adolescent boys and twenty-something losers into impotent, self-indulgent frenzies for fifty years.

"I am the god of hellfire!" the singer boasts. The hell you are.

The murderer pulled out of the parking lot, drove a

few yards, and in a spasm of gunfire, he inexplicably let loose a blast from his shotgun through his windshield and another through the glass of his passenger-side window. Then the tantrum passed, and he once again joined the traffic on the streets of Christchurch. He was a bit more aggressive now—the twenty-eight-year-old killer who has just murdered forty-two people in cold blood honked his horn impatiently at two women who were making their way over a crosswalk a little too slowly for him. But only a bit more aggressive. He still kept well below the speed limit and obeyed every traffic law. You can't be too careful.

In the distance the siren of an emergency vehicle was approaching.

He didn't seem particularly concerned by it. Instead, for the first time since he got into the car uttering the words "Subscribe to PewDiePie" (a reference to a YouTube personality from Sweden with millions of followers who is alleged to have made anti-Semitic comments), the murderer directly addressed what he imagined to be his rapt fans watching his livestream.

First, he expressed surprise—or was it disappointment—that there weren't more women and children killed. He shrugged it off as a minor glitch in his planning. He had overlooked the fact that the women and children tended to show up later than the men for Friday prayers, he explained patiently. But it was slightly later now. Surely there'd be more of them at the next mosque.

"Shit happens," he laughed coldly. And then, in perhaps the most inadvertently self-revealing moment of all, he tries to gaslight his audience, recasting the clumsy fumble of the extended magazine as some kind of heroic moment. "Left one full magazine back there, I know for sure," he intones to the camera, consciously affecting the vocal equivalent of a thousand-yard stare. "Probably more."

"Had to run along in the middle of the firefight and

pick up the mag that fell. Pretty much instantly. There wasn't even time to aim due to so many targets."

Firefight.

Anyone who heard him use that word also knew that he had entered that mosque knowing he had nothing to fear. Because they had watched him do it. They had watched him gun down forty-two unarmed people who offered virtually no resistance. They saw him kill a man who greeted him as a brother with open arms and empty hands. They watched him fire again and again into the bodies of those he had already murdered. And they had watched him shoot a wounded woman in the back. Not a single shot had been fired in return. Not one.

Forget the sixteen-thousand-word manifesto the murderer sent to the prime minister of New Zealand. Everything you need to know about the murderer is in that one word.

Firefight.

There is no silence on earth deeper than the silence between gunshots. It's only human nature that we try to fill it. In the deafening silence in the aftermath of atrocities like the one committed against the people of Christchurch, our first response is to cram whatever we can into the gaping wound to try to stanch the bleeding. Dusty myths and dog-eared narratives, manifestos pecked out in the flickering light of a computer screen in a cheap apartment or a mother's basement, we'll clutch at anything to give meaning to the atrocities, anything that might make sense of the savagery in the hopes that we can know our enemy and combat him, even if it's the grandiose tales the killer tells us and himself to decorate his murderous intent. We forget that the very first sin, the original sin in the Garden of Eden, was not murder: it was grandiosity and selfishness and bitter envy that inhabited one long, scaly coil, followed quickly by lies and self-deception. Only after that litany of sins slithered into the world did the crime of murder follow. Or so it said in that first book on my analyst's bookshelf.

Within hours of the Christchurch massacre the airwaves around the world were pulsing with stories detailing the killer's obsession with immigrants and the extremist views he held, as if that and that alone was what motivated him. We had done the same thing five months earlier, when a reportedly bitter, forty-six-year-old truck driver in Pennsylvania, apparently seeking revenge for his own failures in the world, posted to his racist, anti-Semitic far-right compatriots on the web that he was "going in," as if he were a member of the 82nd Airborne parachuting behind the lines of the Wehrmacht on D-Day.[2] He then stormed into a Pittsburgh synagogue on a Saturday morning to kill eleven Jews at prayer, among them senior citizens and a pair of disabled brothers.

Before that, we assumed we had found an explanation when a young killer waved the Confederate flag in our faces, as if that somehow justified the murders of members of the Bible study group at Emanuel AME Church. Just like the young man at the mosque door in Christchurch, the peaceful prayer group had welcomed the killer inside. And in 2009, when an army psychiatrist—a Muslim about to be deployed to Afghanistan who was described by his fellow soldiers as aloof, belligerent, and paranoid, according to an NPR report at the time[3]—opened fire on his comrades at Fort Hood, many in America accepted his own excuse: he was a jihadist terrorist acting against the policies of the United States when he murdered thirteen people.

Many Americans, among them prominent members of the US Senate, downplayed the idea that it could possibly be anything else and dismissed the possibility that there could have been a complex combination of factors that triggered the psychiatrist's attack. They dismissed the possibility that he was another disturbed employee armed with a newly purchased semiautomatic handgun and a few extended magazines, committing the kind of mass atrocity that is ubiquitous enough in this country that we would have called it "going postal" had it happened in the 1980s or early 1990s at a US post office rather than an army base.

It couldn't possibly be, many Americans believed and continue to believe, that the army major's rampage was sparked by a preexisting and deepening rage and a psychological unraveling, and that jihadism gave his pathology a veneer of reason, a cause. It didn't matter that coworkers would later tell investigators that the psychiatrist, a man reported to have an ego fragile enough to recoil at every perceived slight, had been overwhelmed by the horror stories of the returning veterans he treated, internalizing their stories, seething over them. The horrors of war that his patients had witnessed became all about him, they told investigators. It was beside the point that just like the moody, more depressive of the two killers at Columbine, the psychiatrist had begun to think of suicide, though as Lankford writes in *The Myth of Martyrdom*, he feared the judgment of a God who has fixed his canon against self-slaughter. This prodded him to wrap his suicidal impulses in grandiose visions of mass violence, which at least in his twisted reading of the Quran—a reading reinforced by other apostates on the Internet—was more pleasing to the Almighty.[4]

He certainly wouldn't be the first to bear false witness against the Almighty and try to falsely finger God as a co-conspirator to justify his bloody impulses. History is replete with such tales, from grand mass slaughters by nations in places like Srebrenica to the manic, maladjusted teen at Simon's Rock College in Massachusetts who claimed at trial that God had been whispering to him in the spaces between his synapses, urging him to take a semiautomatic rifle and kill students and teachers at his school in 1992. God has often stood accused of the crimes of men. To the best of my knowledge, He's never directly answered the charges.

It could not be that the root causes of the psychiatrist's rampage were at their core deeply personal and not all that different from the impulses that drove a racist, homophobic, misogynistic murderer from the featureless flatlands between Austin and Waco to drive his pickup truck to a Luby's restaurant in nearby Killeen in 1991, barricade the door with it—just as the killer at West Nickel Mines would later do—and open fire on those inside. He killed twenty-three and wounded twenty-seven, targeting women especially, with a Ruger P89 in one hand, a Glock 17 in the other, shouting as he fired, "All women of Killeen and Belton are vipers! This is what you've done to me and my family! Is it worth it? Tell me, is it worth it?"[5]

No. We tell ourselves that there's a hard line between those we call terrorists, who act under cover of some grand political or cultural or religious cause, and those among us who kill for their own perverse personal reasons, though, as Lankford tells us, the line is seldom as hard and fast as that.

To their credit, against a wave of public opposition and in the teeth of a resolution by the Senate dubbing the attack "the worst act of terrorism on US soil since September 11, 2001," neither the US Army nor the president at the time bowed to the psychiatrist's insistence that he was anything more than a mass murderer.[6]

The Department of Defense officially listed the 2009 Fort Hood shooting as a case of "workplace violence." The killer, who had graduated from Virginia Tech ten years before the massacre there, was not charged under federal terrorism statutes. Instead, he was convicted by court-martial of thirteen counts of premeditated murder and thirty-two counts of attempted murder, and he was sentenced to death. As of this writing he is still being held in the military prison at Fort Leavenworth, Kansas, where he still insists he's some kind of martyr to a cause. The order of execution will not endorse that claim.

None of this is to suggest that the killer at Fort Hood did not see himself as a terrorist, although he probably wouldn't use that particular word. He did indeed haunt websites and chat rooms in the darkest corners of the Internet where jihadists are recruited and groomed. As he sank into deeper rage and increasingly embraced an operatic fantasy of his own demise, one in which he could see himself as a martyr, he saw every injury against him, real or imagined, small or large, through that prism, as part of an assault on Muslims writ large. He had—perhaps always—been so inclined. When, toward the end of his medical training, his fellow health professionals in the military failed to show what he believed was proper deference to a droning report he delivered, "The Koranic World View as It Relates to Muslims in the U.S. Military," it wasn't his writing, his research, or his style they were disrespecting, it was all of Islam.[7]

In time it appears the psychiatrist, who despite his Palestinian descent spoke virtually no Arabic, had become, in his mind, an avatar for the whole of the Muslim universe. When his car was keyed—allegedly by a solider who was indeed, a neighbor said, hostile to the psychiatrist's religion—he filed that away as another attack on the whole of the Muslim world, another data point on a continuum that ran the gamut from petty vandalism to all-out war. And he did have several contacts with Anwar al-Awlaki, a onetime moderate Muslim cleric who, like the psychiatrist, had lived in Virginia before he transformed himself into the so-called "Bin Laden of the Internet."[8] Army investigators later concluded that the contacts were made in connection with legitimate research the psychiatrist was doing; and before he was killed in an American drone strike in 2011, al-Aw-laki himself, in an interview with the Yemeni journalist Abdulelah Hider Shaea that was later reported by the *Washington Post*, denied that he had directed the psychiatrist to attack his fellow soldiers at Fort Hood.[9] But then again, he didn't really need to.

Our shadowy adversaries across the globe have learned how to exploit one of our Achilles' heels, our lax gun laws. A 2017 article in the official magazine of ISIS, for example, urged its followers to visit American gun shows, exercise their Second Amendment rights, and wait for the opportunity to use them against us.[10] They have also learned to exploit another of our Achilles' heels. It's that peculiar, toxic cocktail of grievance and grandiosity, of victimhood-as-status, that sociologists Campbell and Manning write about. It's a combination found in abundance in the societies that can afford it, in the affluent—our adversaries would call it decadent—West, where there's a perhaps unrealistic expectation of personal success and an incentive to view one's self as a victim when that success proves elusive.

Inside their echo chambers on the Internet, the disturbed, the isolated, the wrathful—usually but not exclusively white men who believe their primacy and privilege are being eroded by the modest gains of women or minorities or immigrants or non-cisgendered people—can pick and choose from a vast menu of Others to blame for what they see as their diminished status, says Casey Kelly, author of *Apocalypse Man: The Death Drive and the Rhetoric of White Masculine Victimhood*.[11] Inside those echo chambers they can take on the mantle of a savior, a martyr, a dark hero to some twisted cause. And they will be encouraged to do so. Praised for it. Celebrated for it.

"Men are not gentle creatures who want to be loved, and who at the most can defend themselves if they are attacked," Freud writes in *Civilization and Its*

Discontents, that second book on my analyst's bookshelf. "They are, on the contrary, creatures among whose instinctual endowments is to be reckoned a powerful share of aggressiveness."[12]

Inside the echo chambers of extremism of any stripe, bitterness is a virtue, and the more aggressively it's displayed, the more highly those who gather in those low places regard each other. And they gather there by the score. These virtual places serve as magnets for the angry, for those with little success to point to in the real world, for those with festering envy and a grandiose sense of themselves. These websites gather once-isolated loners from all over the nation, indeed from across the world.

Take the truck driver from Pittsburgh, a guy whose estranged father had committed suicide after being charged with rape and whose stepfather, it seems, had been accused of similar offenses, according to a deeply researched profile of him done by the *Pittsburgh Post-Gazette* after the massacre at Tree of Life synagogue in 2018. A high school dropout—he never finished his senior year, the *Post-Gazette* reported—he eventually drifted into a low-paying job driving a truck for a local bakery and later quit that to become an even more isolated over-the-road truck driver.[13] Back then he would drape himself in a borrowed dignity, the paper reported. Whenever he had a task to complete, the truck driver, who had never served a day in uniform, would affect a faux military bearing and snap, "I'm going in"—the same words he used before beginning his attack at Tree of Life.

This man who barely made a ripple in the real world found a way to make himself seem important in a virtual one. At least in his own eyes. His gateway drug was a local far-right talk-radio program called *The WarRoom*, a conspiracy-minded broadcast that still today fans the smoldering resentments of its listeners with tales of a grand plot by the "blue hats" of the United Nations to subjugate the world. He had started listening in the 1990s, and by the time he was in his late twenties, he had earned himself the title of unofficial archivist for the program. But that was all he earned. As the manager of the company that ran the broadcast back then told the *Post-Gazette*, they never considered putting him on the payroll. The host of the broadcast later told the *Washington Post* that he had no recollection of ever having even met the truck driver.[14]

He also seems to have found status in his own eyes through firearms. According to the *Post-Gazette*, he spent considerable time at a local rifle range in the state game lands, and he apparently imagined himself—as these killers so often do—as a gunslinging hero facing off against some operatic threat from a globalist horde. The paper quoted one acquaintance who recalled that he used to imagine invaders coming at him in body armor and helmets and practiced leveling his shotgun at what he imagined would be face level to make sure that he killed his make-believe adversaries.

And as the years passed, whenever he wasn't on the range or on the road, it seemed this high school dropout who imagined himself to be a seasoned lone warrior was on the net, haunting far-right websites. He favored the kind of festering sites where the ever-thin line between fears of some global elite taking over the world and the outright anti-Semitism that fantasy often masks vanishes altogether. Studies have shown that in recent years such websites have proliferated, and their impact is predictable: in one year alone, from 2016 to 2017, the number of anti-Semitic incidents spiked by nearly 60 percent.[15]

In the weeks leading up to the killings, the truck driver—and perhaps millions of other Americans who shared his overheated fear of foreigners—had been whipped into a frenzy. The president of the United States, who had staked his election campaign on stoking fears of an invasion of migrants and refugees on our southern border, albeit in less blatantly anti-Semitic terms, now claimed that a "caravan" of migrants was making its way across Mexico toward the United States. He signaled that these hungry, sometimes shoeless families of migrants should be treated as a military threat.

In the dark corners of the web where the Tree of Life killer spent his days, in those places where the ubiquitous sense of grievance and resentment and fear now openly embraced in our culture is distilled down to its toxic essence, the "threat" of the "caravan" was taken seriously. For the truck driver, it seems, it created a perfect vertical alignment of all of the grudges he bore. Globalists in the thrall of internationalist Jews were fomenting an invasion, he believed, and they were using the Hebrew Immigrant Aid Society, a respected one-hundred-year-old nonprofit that has eased the transition for many legal immigrants since the days of pickle barrels and schmatta shops on Delancey Street. From there it was a short step to his fixation on the Tree of Life synagogue, a formidable building on a tree-lined street in the Squirrel Hill section of town where Fred Rogers had once lived—the real Mr. Rogers's neighborhood—shared by three branches of Judaism. It's not at all clear that the Tree of Life killer cared about the distinctions among them. They were Jews, and in his twisted fantasy world their goal was to diminish him. Personally. They were props in his own grandiose drama, a drama in which he was the "good guy with a gun" standing up to invading hordes.

Whatever his failures, whatever bad cards life had dealt him, and however badly he may have played them, at least he was a middle-aged white man in a country where, in his mind, that meant he was entitled to something, and that entitlement was being threatened. He might have little to distinguish himself in the real world, but in the virtual world he could claim to be an avenger, a warrior, without fear of being challenged or ridiculed. Rather, he would be lionized as he no doubt believed was his due.

In truth, his resentments and grudges, his willingness to kill, and his conviction that doing so would grant him a status that seems to have otherwise eluded him may not have been all that different from the petty resentments of a sixty-one-year-old junk dealer who turned active shooter in 2013. About to be evicted from his home, a shed with a bucket for a toilet on a trash-strewn piece of property not far from my home in northeastern Pennsylvania, he had racked up thousands of dollars in unpaid fines for using his land as a trash heap. The municipality had condemned his land and had ordered him to vacate when he stormed into a municipal committee meeting in Ross Township armed with a Ruger Mini-14 semiautomatic rifle and a handgun and murdered three people before he was tackled and restrained by an unarmed municipal employee. At his sentencing—he was ordered to serve three consecutive life sentences for murder—he spent forty minutes railing about how he was a "victim" of a "conspiracy" that had been launched against him when he was ordered to clean up his yard.[16]

I got a glimpse into the Ross Township killer's mindset in 2017 when I wrote him a letter trying to arrange an interview in prison. In his multipage response, he made it clear that he believed that his murders had given him some sort of unearned celebrity and status, and he set forth a list of demands, including specific amounts of money I needed to deposit into his prison commissary account before I would be granted the honor of an interview. I wasn't going to waste a stamp telling him to go to hell. I didn't need to. Pretty much every question I had, the junkman had answered with that letter.

To the extent that there was any difference at all between the killer in Ross Township and the murderer at

Tree of Life, it was that the killer in Pittsburgh reached for a more elaborate justification when he reached for his rifle, and he chose his targets for what they represented in his mind rather than what they had allegedly done to him personally.

Just before the massacre, the Tree of Life killer posted one last time on the Internet. On one of the fringe social media sites he frequented most often, he wrote, "HIAS likes to bring invaders in to kill our people. I can't sit by and watch my people get slaughtered. Screw your optics."[17]

He signed off with the same faux-militaristic phrase he'd used when he was ordered to load a tray of hot cross buns into the back of his truck, back in the days when he still hauled bread for the bakery.

"I'm going in," he wrote. He had loaded his legally purchased Colt AR-15 in his rental car, as well as the shotgun he'd used to fantasize about face shots to blue-helmeted globalists. He'd leave that shotgun in the car because he knew no one inside the shul on an early Shabbos morning would be wearing body armor or helmets. He also had three .357 Glock handguns when he climbed into the car, headed off toward the synagogue, and pulled into a handicapped parking space.

I have no idea whether he engaged the emergency brake.

As the number of casualties of mass public shootings has spiked in recent years, and as the research into the minds of these murderers has evolved, the mass media has, by and large, gotten wise to the fact that a thirst for glory and self-aggrandizement is at least one of the factors that drives these killers. They want to be famous in a culture that, as discussed earlier, often prizes fame above all else. In that, they're just like the rest of us. Only more so. In response, it's become standard practice in the media to downplay the killer's name and to focus instead on the lives that these killers snuffed out. That's a good thing.

But here's a troubling question. Do we risk making a similar mistake when we accept on their face and almost without question the claims of some perverse political motives made by these killers?

To be sure, there is a political dimension to the claims made by some of these shooters. As one of the early readers of this manuscript noted, "If inflammatory political rhetoric stokes a shooter's paranoia/anger/psychosis as he shoots up a synagogue or a Walmart in a border city, certainly the impact of his actions matter just as much, if not more, than what was going on in his head."

Perhaps.

There is no question that the swamps these killers swim in darkly reflect troubling aspects of our political culture: the angst felt primarily by white males who see themselves as losing status against the comparatively modest gains made by women and people of color and other groups. Nor is there any question that their anger has been stoked by a political culture that has sought to commoditize their angst.

It cannot be stated strongly enough that the casualties in many of these attacks were targeted because of who they were and what they represented in the killers' twisted and stunted philosophies. Jews died because they were Jews. Hispanics were murdered because of their ethnic heritage. Women were killed because they were not men. The killer psychiatrist at Fort Hood may not have been a soldier in a global struggle, but the people the psychiatrist murdered—soldiers in uniform, on active duty—certainly died while defending their country.

The killer at Poway, in San Diego—who also wrote a rambling, juvenile manifesto in which he cloaked himself in verses from the Bible and the white supremacist playbook—and the murderer at Tree of Life may have wanted the world to see them as victims of some international conspiracy, but is their justification any more real or based in fact than the so-called conspiracy by a township committee to get the junkman to throw out the trash he had accumulated?

At their core, they share at least one thing in common, a trait that transcends the readily available political causes that they espouse. What they share is a sense of themselves as victims and a narcissistic image of themselves as armed avengers, destined for some perverse fame.

Victims.

It's ironic that the Jews who survived the attacks at Pittsburgh and Poway, members of a people who have actually been targeted by real conspiracies at least since their neighbors in Egypt conspired to drive them out of Alexandria more than two thousand years ago, most emphatically do not act like victims.

In the late spring of 2019, a killer who claimed to be inspired by the murderer from Christchurch and the killer from Pittsburgh opened fire at the Chabad synagogue in Poway, killing a sixty-year-old woman and wounding three people, among them an eight-year-old child and the rabbi, whose hand was mangled by a bullet. Just days after that attack, the congregation presented the rabbi with a gift, a yad, a Torah pointer that had been purchased almost on a whim by a member of his congregation months earlier. It was modified so he could overcome his injury and continue to intone the ancient verses.

Hannah Kaye, the daughter of Lori Gilbert-Kaye, the only fatality in that attack, could easily have focused on the horror of it—her father, a physician, had rushed to perform CPR on the wounded woman and collapsed, a witness told me. He collapsed when he realized that it was his wife he was frantically trying to revive.

Yet Hannah Kaye had just barely gotten up from sitting shiva—the traditional seven-day mourning period among Jews—when the Internet and social media lit up with her joyous celebration of her mother's life, praising her as an *eshet chayil*, a Righteous Woman who embodies the eternal virtues commanded in the Torah: generosity and humility, courage and faithfulness. It had been Lori who had purchased the yad, a congregant told me. There's a magnificent defiance in that.

Dean Root, a congregant at the Tree of Life who had just arrived at the synagogue as the shooting began and who provided sanctuary in his car to at least one person fleeing the massacre, told me that in the wake of the attack, the three often-bickering sibling strands of Judaism that shared the building became more united. Their adherents rededicated themselves to the core values of their shared faith, he told me, not the least of which is the obligation to care for the stranger in your midst, embodied by the work of the Hebrew Immigrant Aid Society. That daily victory over darkness, that refusal to claim the mantle of victim was also trumpeted on the web.

I hope that galls the hell out of the murderer.

These devotees are not alone in refusing victimhood. Indeed, as we'll see in chapter 9, at least since Sandy Hook, the survivors of mass shootings—and those touched by them—have increasingly used the same technology the killers use to stoke their murderous impulses. They use the same technology that lionizes the killers and even amplifies the impact of their crimes, broadcasting them in real time to people all over the nation and the world, to announce to the world that they have indeed survived. More than that, organizations like Everytown for Gun Safety, Rep. Gabby Giffords's foundation, and the March for Our Lives (established by the survivors of the Parkland massacre in Florida) have tried to turn the virtual sword the killers wielded into a million digital plowshares, using the Internet to build support for initiatives that they hope might combat the epidemic of gun violence in this country.

That light may never make it down to the depths of the web where the damaged vessels dwell that serve as incubators for these killers. But it's a start.

And it's worth remembering that these websites did not make the killers out of whole cloth. In many cases they brought the cloth themselves, and in those parts of the web they got help turning them into costumes. As Lankford writes in *The Myth of Martyrdom*, even if the Virginia-born psychiatrist at Fort Hood had not been a Muslim, had not found a sense of belonging among other wannabe jihadists on the web, even if he had been a Christian or a Jew, "he would still have had severe personal problems and the inability to handle them."

"He would just have attacked somewhere else instead."[18]

Regardless of what they tell themselves. Regardless of what we tell ourselves.

Of course, these killers, depending on their own identities, are drawn to the hate-filled websites of Islamic extremism or to the flickering torches of the white supremacist movement and gravitate to the websites that these racists wallow in. Those places are cesspools of self-pity, and that perceived sense of victimhood is a defining characteristic of mass shooters, the experts like Lankford, Meloy, and Kelly tell us.

Inside the imaginary walls of these electronic medieval cities that defy borders and span the globe, guys like the Christchurch shooter, who barely warrant a glance in the real world, can fashion themselves as kings. They can give full rein to their grandiosity and imagine themselves as twisted heroes out of some stunted adolescent version of an ancient nationalist saga.

Those sites provide them succor and cover and offer

whole identities that they can refine to reinforce their own murderous peculiarities.

And for that, all of those who gather there are culpable for every death at Christchurch and Pittsburgh and Poway and Charleston and Fort Hood. But it would be a stretch to imagine that they made these killers out of nothing. These criminals, in many cases, almost certainly had the makings of killers long before they ever found those sites.

"I should have been that I am, had the maidenliest star in the firmament twinkled on my bastardizing," the villain Edmond says in act 1, scene 2 of *King Lear*, in that third book on my analyst's bookshelf.

As I said before: maybe I was wrong. Maybe that shrink all those years ago was onto something.

Chapter 5

Jokers Wild

D IE, Commie dogs!" he bleats as he squeezes off round after round from a semiautomatic rifle, sending his bullets into a loose grouping at what would more or less be the head and torso of a man-shaped target. "That's right!" his pudgy, middle-aged sidekick squeals in a raspy, high-pitched voice that sounds like he's been gargling with thumbtacks. "Right in the head!"

As you watch this live-streaming event, you can almost smell the gun smoke through the screen, and you might imagine that you could catch a whiff of musky cologne and the scent of hair gel, leavened with perhaps just a hint of over-the-counter testosterone boosters. Sure, the pudgy sidekick has ticked off a list of enemies for the camera before heading onto the range:

"the Democrats and Antifa and George Soros and the *New York Times*," and lest we forget, some guy who, he says, once dumped a cup of coffee over his head. Over his shoulder a smattering of cheap tinsel glistens on an anemic *tannenbaum*, as if to remind us that these two are also prepared to lay down their lives if need be in the war on Christmas.

Sure, they drone on about a looming possible civil war and about how they and Americans like them are under assault by some global conspiracy—the "corporate Clinton conspiracy," the sidekick dubbed it. But there's no reason to imagine that either of these guys is ever likely to do anything other than talk. That's what they do for a living. Talk.

For years, the sidekick had curated a public image of himself as a conspiracy-minded agitator, filling the airwaves and social media with one unhinged rant after another—all, he would later claim in court papers, in service of the character he was playing for his hardcore, easily deceived audience. His way-over-the-top antics had earned him a couple of lawsuits and, when he declared the Sandy Hook massacre a hoax, a false-flag operation designed to trick Americans into giving up their Second Amendment rights, the lasting enmity of every cop in America who has ever had to respond to a mass public shooting. Within hours of the attack his rants goaded his gullible followers into unleashing a hateful barrage of despicable emails, texts, and phone calls to the parents of the children murdered at Newtown.

But no matter.

He had created a niche in the market and filled it, building a career by playing the sputtering loudmouth who is ever present at the end of every bar in America, fleshy fists clenching, ready to pick a fight with anybody who has to pass near him on the way to the pissoir. He would milk that role for all it was worth for more than a decade, until at last the famously hands-off powers that be that lord it over social media had enough of his unfounded, conspiratorial braying and banned him.

His companion, clearly the top banana in this particular burlesque, had also spent decades creating a theatrical public persona as both a political provocateur and a fastidious dandy. He had once appeared on the cover of an alternative-lifestyle magazine dressed in leather, baring his back at one point during the photo shoot to reveal a tattoo of the face of his former boss, disgraced president Richard Nixon, beaming beatifically from between his shoulder blades. More often, though, he liked to appear on the pages of magazines and newspapers and websites in gaudy suits: pinstripes the size of highway lane lines or alabaster white suits that set off his carefully coiffed mane of white hair and complemented his oversized, owl-eyed round spectacles. With his flamboyant ties and pocket squares, his tanning-bed tan and his crafted air of naughty insouciance, he conjured an image of a taller Roy Cohn with better hair, perpetually dressed for a dinner party at Dr. Frank-N-Furter's castle in Denton where meatloaf will be served.

Over a long and provocative career as a political dirty trickster, he gleefully cultivated a reputation as a guy whose deeds were as outlandish as his dress. In 2019, for example, while free on bail awaiting trial on charges that grew out of the Mueller investigation into Russian interference in the 2016 election, charges that he insisted were all part of that grand global conspiracy his sidekick had referred to, the top banana posted a picture to his followers online of the judge in that case with a gunsight crosshairs beside her face. When the judge became understandably upset, he claimed, through his attorneys, that the gunsight was actually a Celtic cross. Maybe he didn't know that the Celtic cross is a symbol that's been appropriated in recent years by the white nationalist movement. Or maybe he did and was just hoping that the judge, who is Jewish, did not.

Today, the top banana seems to be trying to channel Illya Kuryakin, the heartthrob Russian agent from the old 1960s *Man from U.N.C.L.E.* television series, with a black turtleneck and a lethal-looking semiautomatic to match. Over the course of the next hour or so, the top banana and his sidekick fire off round after round, aiming at the two-dimensional outline of an imaginary enemy that looks no more threatening than a bowling pin. They're cackling like high school boys as they shoot. "We're so scared of Antifa," the sidekick says with mock bravado as he squeezes off a burst from a rifle on full automatic.

They're like kids in a candy store, if that candy store were located somewhere on Hogan's Alley, the simulated urban street at Quantico where FBI agents are trained to know when to shoot and when not to.

"Hey! Can I get one of these?" the sidekick trills to the range master as he picks up a particularly menacing-looking weapon. It's black, of course, with a rifle stock long enough to compensate for its grotesquely short barrel. "I like this better than the Vector," he says, referring to another semiautomatic recognizable in profile by a paunch of a receiver that dwarfs its undersized barrel.

With their every word, their every move, the top banana and his sidekick radiate an in-your-face adolescent fake swagger. It doesn't fit them well at their age. But they're working it. Mugging for the camera. They seem to be consciously acting for their audience—and overacting at that. Feverishly trying to trigger more than a barrage of bullets with each pull, they're clearly hoping to trigger liberals all over the country.

In that, they pretty much failed. Apart from some forced pearl-clutching over at the reliably liberal online outlet Media Matters and similar sites on that end of the political spectrum, most Americans took no note at all of the video.[1] Those few who did by and large saw it for what it was: a stunt, a typically overwrought American sideshow designed to entertain a particular American audience that has gawked at such sideshows since the days when the Internet was nothing more than two tin cans connected by Al Gore, and even before that.

Of course, somewhere down in the deepest reaches of the net there might have been some benighted souls who took these two burlesque comics seriously. For the most part, to the degree that they were even aware of the video, most Americans, right or left, wrote it off as just two more middle-aged white jokers adding their static to the white noise over guns and victimhood and some cartoonish version of manhood that has always been in the background of this culture.

* * *

There's an adolescent giddiness in the crisp spring air. You can practically smell it wafting off the screen as you watch the video. It mixes with the acrid stench of gun smoke and the sound of gunfire echoing off the trees and the rocks at Rampart Range, a beautiful, secluded corner of a national park in the Rocky Mountains in Colorado.

There are five young people there, four of them males. One of them brought his girlfriend with him, along with a cache of mean-looking weapons. There's an illegal sawed-off shotgun "straight out of *Doom*," one of them would later boast, referring to a violent video game he played from time to time, and a Hi-Point 995 carbine, one of a type of weapon that had been manufactured specifically to blast through the holes in the 1994 assault weapons ban. There's a TEC-9, a semiautomatic handgun that had been banned, but because there were plenty of them in circulation, they were still easy to obtain without attracting any undue attention at gun shows, as this one had been, or on the secondhand market. Easy enough that a couple of underage suburban kids with no real underworld connections could get their hands on one as easily as they could get a bottle of cheap vodka or a pack of cigarettes. Just get somebody over eighteen to stroll in and buy it for you.

Which is what they had done.

They brought other weapons with them, too, and a lot of ammunition, as well as a few bowling pins stolen from a local alley to use as targets.

And, of course, a camcorder to memorialize it all.

All four of the males appear to be consciously working their swagger for the camera, especially the two younger ones. Both are still seventeen, both still wearing the matching, oversized black trench coats they had donned that morning to guard against the chill, the sort of trench coats that would soon enough play an oversize role in American mythology, though they'll shed them later in the day as they work up a sweat.

They're doing their best to come off as four Mickeys and one Mallory, characters from their favorite movie of the era, the gory comic-book paean to American carnage, *Natural Born Killers*. It's a movie that purports to be a satirical critique of America's obsession with mass violence. But instead it wallows in it, casting its two psychopathic antiheroes as a latter-day Bonnie and Clyde; it's a manic film that hits its blood-soaked climax in one cataclysmic explosion of mayhem when the two avenging dark angels, dressed all in white, reap the souls of those who they—and the audience—deem unfit to live. The film was the number-one hit in America the weekend it opened in 1994, grossing the equivalent of what would today be about $20 million in its first three days, and it remained a blockbuster at Blockbuster for years after that. And the two heavily armed, trench-coated teens were among its biggest fans.

At one point, after unleashing a barrage of fire at a target, the smaller of the younger teens, the one who clearly sees himself as the alpha-mad-dog in this little pack, picks up the bullet- and pellet-riddled bowling pin to admire his handiwork.

There's a loose grouping of holes more or less where the head and torso of the vaguely human-shaped target would be, with one particularly large hole near the top. "Entry wound, exit wound," he says gleefully, twirling the bowling pin, taking care to make sure the camera focuses on the gaping holes.

None of them are at all proficient with the weapons.

In fact, when the more sullen of the two trench-coat-clad teens lets loose with a blast from the sawed-off shotgun, he's completely unprepared for the recoil. It injures his wrist and draws a bit of blood. The same thing happens to the alpha-mad-dog when he tries the gun. Though he quickly changes his stance to adapt, he still ends up with a bloody scrape on his grip hand. He mugs for the camera and appears to spank the offending shotgun.

"When high school kids use guns," someone says, just off camera, and all five of them fill the silence between gunshots with peals of laughter.

Months after the April 20, 1999, mass shooting at Columbine High School, there was widespread alarm when word of the tape of this armed escapade in the woods first surfaced, along with the disclosure that there was a cache of recordings that came to be known as the "Basement Tapes" that augmented the killers' journals and scribblings. Surely these electronic documents were all red flags that sent an unmistakable warning of the murders to come. Indeed, though the Basement Tapes themselves were never released—the local sheriff's department eventually destroyed them, twelve years after the mass shooting—they were shown to a reporter from *Time* magazine.[2] They've been well documented and do detail the elaborate way the pair plotted the massacre over the course of a year. And they provide a glimpse into their motive and their inspiration.

It wasn't about bullying. They weren't members of some subterranean goth subculture or an imaginary Trench Coat Mafia. The trench coats, it turned out, were nothing more than a handy way to hide their weapons, and they shed them early in the attack. They weren't gunning specifically for Christians or African Americans or gay people or jocks.

In fact, as the detailed description of the content of the tapes shows, they weren't gunning for anybody in particular. Yes, a couple of their schoolmates are singled out by name in the tapes, but not one of those named would be targeted during the actual assault, as Dave Cullen, the chronicler of Columbine, has noted. And, yes, the self-appointed leader of the duo would tick off a list of the usual targets: women, African Americans, Hispanics, gay people, and Jews, as his half-Jewish co-conspirator signaled his assent.

But, like their trench coats, it's clear from the transcripts that those targets only cloaked their real objective.

What they wanted more than anything, FBI psychologists, profilers, and analysts would later conclude, was the fame—or infamy—that they were certain would come in the aftermath of what they imagined to be a slaughter on a cinematic scale. They weren't hoping just to gun down a few of their schoolmates, or more. As Cullen writes, at one point the alpha-mad-dog even sarcastically dismisses the shooters in then-recent attacks in Kentucky and Jonesboro, Arkansas, as "those fucks . . . with camouflage and .22s."

Instead, their self-aggrandizing plot was intended to murder every single person in the building with an array of propane bombs in a cataclysmic explosion of mayhem that would, in their minds, dwarf what was then the mostly deadly terrorist attack on US soil, the Oklahoma City bombing. "I hope we kill 250 of you," the more sullen of the pair says, boasting later that he expects their rampage will exact "the most deaths in U.S. history." The guns were only intended to announce the beginning of the attack and to mow down survivors. They dubbed their plot "NBK," an homage and maybe a challenge to their favorite movie, even though they expected that their murderous exploits would eclipse those of their make-believe antiheroes, Mickey and Mallory.

In that, they failed.

The killers' utter ineptitude with bomb-making techniques meant that all of the bombs they had planted—one across town to create a diversion and several more in the high school cafeteria meant to collapse the building—either fizzled or didn't ignite at all.

That was when the Columbine massacre became a mass public shooting.

We know now, as FBI analysts have concluded, that the smaller of the two was a classic psychopath, nothing more intriguing or extraordinary than that. We know that his sullen co-conspirator was a sometimes-combustible depressive bent on committing suicide, a self-absorbed teen moonstruck enough to whimper rhapsodically about how romantic love had eluded him, yet cold and cruel and narcissistic enough to demand that thirteen innocent people, most of them his schoolmates, die with him when he did himself in.[3]

We now know what they did, and we know the perverse reasons they did it.

And if you choose to become one of the hundreds of thousands of people who have viewed one of the few surviving tapes made by the Columbine killers on YouTube, the one that documents their armed escapade at Rampart Range, you'll almost certainly see it as a terrifying foreshadow of what was to come.

But here's a thought exercise. Suppose, for a moment, that the transcripts of the rest of the tapes had never been made public and this was the only tape you saw or heard about. Suppose further that the technology existed at the time that would allow you to view it before the atrocity at Columbine was committed. Would you have concluded that these were mass murderers in waiting? Or would you have written them off as testosterone-poisoned boys aping the antiheroes from their favorite shoot-'em-up, mugging for the camera and for the only female in their group?

Would you pay them any more heed than you might a scrawny kid in the lobby of a Connecticut movie theater working himself into a sweaty frenzy as he played *Dance Dance Revolution*?

Or suppose it's sometime before midnight on July 20, 2012, and you happen to be in Aurora, Colorado, some sixteen miles from Columbine, when you catch a glimpse of an unusually pale young man with garish orange dye in his hair; he's dressed in off-the-rack black tactical gear and making his way to the Century 16 movie theater for the late-night showing of the uber-violent *Dark Knight Rises*.

Would you assume that he was a mentally unstable killer going there to kill twelve people and wound fifty-eight by gunfire? Or would your first guess have been that he was just a superfan of the Joker and the overwrought violent entertainments that feature him?

Would you have seen him as a reincarnation of the Columbine killers? Or would he have looked like just another eager fan of the bloody thrillers that have been the stock-in-trade of the American movie industry since its beginning and the stuff of pulp novels long before that, the kind of stuff we flock to by the millions?

Would he have struck you as being different in anything but style from the two middle-aged jokers playing

Rambo and mugging for the camera in Austin five years later?

"Right in the head!" the paunchy sidekick squeals in that tape from Austin, in a high-pitched voice that sounds like he's been gargling with thumbtacks.

Maybe we're hearing it wrong. Maybe "right in the head" isn't a giddy ejaculation after all. Maybe it's a question. And maybe it's a question that applies to all of us.

* * *

There's a brief but deep silence on the other end of the phone line, and I can almost hear him trying to build an answer to my question, an answer big enough to fill it.

"Would 'a good guy with a gun' have stopped you?" I had asked.

As he gathered his thoughts, I gathered mine.

I had started this series of lengthy telephone chats with more than a few second thoughts. One survivor of his heinous crime had told me in no uncertain terms that she believed this murderer to be a glory-seeking, unreconstructed killer and nothing more, a narcissist still basking in the media attention his rampage had brought him more than twenty-five years after he murdered her mentor, Ñacuñán Sáez, and her classmate, Galen Gibson, and wounded four others at Simon's Rock College in Massachusetts. He remains a shrewdly intuitive con man, she told me, still trying to manipulate gullible reporters into granting him the fame he desperately craves, still trying to position himself in the murderer's row of mass public shooters, despite the fact that his botched rampage had left just two dead.

Perhaps it's a measure of what we've become that "just" two lives taken—one marked by service, the other full of boundless potential—merits inclusion on that list only with an asterisk.

That's a distinction without a difference, Anne Thalheimer tells me. It was only the murderer's ineptitude—he had clumsily tried to modify his cheap, Chinese-made AK-47 knockoff to fire faster and in the process made sure that it wouldn't fire at all after a few rounds— that prevented him from claiming far more lives. "Man, if that gun had worked the way he wanted it to, he would have killed all of us," she said.

And yet, the way she sees it, he's been granted a platform that no murderer deserves.

After Virginia Tech, a reporter from *Newsweek* called him, she reminds me, to ask the Taiwanese-born murderer for his take on the case. What he took, she says, was credit for being that killer's inspiration, though there's no evidence in the videos or writings left by the Virginia Tech shooter that he took any note of the Simon's Rock murderer at all. "[He] was just very much like, 'Yeah, I inspired that. Oh yeah, Asian American shooters are like super rare.'"

What he actually said was somewhat less overtly boastful: "At first I thought it was just a coincidence," he told the reporter from *Newsweek*,

> but as more details came out, there were just too many eerie similarities to me. He was an immigrant, like myself. The events leading up to the shooting, the warning signs he gave out really reminded me of what happened at Simon's Rock. They said he had mental-health issues. I don't really think I had mental-health issues, but I did give out those warning signs. He harassed women, and I also had an incident where I was accused of stalking a female classmate. He went and purchased a gun at a store 40 minutes out of town; so did I. He wrote papers that got people's attention; I did that, too.[4]

Thalheimer's point was taken.

Beyond that mass-media notoriety breathlessly awarded to him by a press eager to fill the airwaves and their websites and their first editions with his hot takes on the latest example of a particular atrocity, he has also been rewarded for his crime by popular culture. As I mentioned earlier, the band Weezer had recorded a song in his honor—a "lullaby," they called it—that plays fast and loose with the facts of the slaying. In many respects, it's a different version of the same tune that's been playing in the background ever since Kinky Friedman penned his ballad to the failed Marine murderer in Austin, different in style but not in substance. In their ode, Weezer timidly laments the murders while casting the murderer as a kind of sympathetic, moody antihero: an outcast and a rebel overwhelmed by a sense of betrayal as his school chums slink ignominiously toward the stifling conformity of adulthood.

In the years since its release, the song has gotten modest airplay from time to time, and it's earned a certain cachet among a small subset of Weezer fans.

Thalheimer is not among them.

The way she sees it, there's something perverse in trading a moment of airtime or a drop of ink for the blood the murderer spilled. "I don't see him as a sympathetic figure," she says. "And I don't think it's fair for him to get sympathetic airtime."

There are others touched by the murders at Simon's Rock who see things somewhat differently than Thalheimer. But only somewhat. Among them is Galen's father, Greg Gibson. In the years since the slayings, Greg Gibson developed an unusual connection—relationship is too strong a word; association might be a better fit—with his son's murderer. In letters and in person the two have spoken often. They remain in touch.

It's a unique enough association that it has attracted national media attention. NPR and other outlets have reported on it, depicting it as a search for understanding, with perhaps a spirit of forgiveness hovering in the background. Greg Gibson indulges no such gauzy fantasies in his own book, *Gone Boy: A Walkabout*, his piercing and brutally honest account of his life after his son's death, and in his conversation with me, Gibson makes it clear that to him the association is strictly mercantile. His goal is not to understand the murderer—he believes he does understand him. "He was fucking crazy," he tells me. "You've got to be crazy to kill somebody, don't you?"

And it's certainly not about forgiveness: not in the Amish sense of the word, not in any sense of the word.

"I don't believe in forgiveness," he tells me matter-of-factly. "I don't understand what it is. It's some kind of word you hear on TV. But I don't know what forgiveness is. The only sense of forgiveness I have is, 'I, on high, the mighty wronged one, forgive you, you little worm . . . who wronged me.'"

"I choose not be interested in that whatsoever."

Nor is he oblivious to the fact that sometimes-fawning news coverage over his association with the killer risks reopening old wounds for others in the awful fraternity of those damaged emotionally or physically by the Simon's Rock murders and other mass slayings.

He knows that because he's been told. Thalheimer has told him.

She remembers being in graduate school, years after the slayings, still trying to keep the ordeal she had survived from her colleagues, only to have the whole horrible event come flooding back when the morning paper was delivered.

"I didn't really tell anybody in grad school what I had gone through, because how do you work that into a conversation?" she says. In the aftermath of the murders, she had, in ways large and small, modified her behavior: "Like I'm gonna sit in this room but I need to make sure

I know where all the exits are, and I can't have my back to the door because that's gonna freak me out."

"All these particular things kind of just become second nature," she says, and she did them with a forced nonchalance to keep from drawing attention to herself. "You know, you can do that in such a way that people don't notice that that's what you're doing," she says.

And I came in one day, and on the cover of the *New York Times* there's a picture of Greg Gibson, there's a picture of [the murderer], and it's front-page news about how they're talking to each other. And I'm like, "ARE YOU SERIOUS RIGHT NOW?"

My personal hell is on the cover of the *New York Times*. And in so many ways, that has become sort of the overriding narrative of Simon's Rock. It has become less and less about Galen and Ñacuñán and more and more about Greg and [the killer].

It's not that Greg Gibson is insensitive to all of that. He understands the collateral damage that his association with the murderer can do. It's just that he also believes it's worth it, that by mining the killer's story and entering into an uneasy alliance with him, he can use him to advance his now quarter-century-long campaign to find ways to prevent future mass slayings. "This is a transactional deal," he tells me. "I don't have any moral investment. . . . I'm working with him to make a product that I hope will have some effect on reducing gun violence. That simple."

A rare-book dealer by trade, Greg Gibson has a peddler's sixth sense, a natural suspicion of anything that anybody tells him. He's always on the lookout for a con. And even he can't tell for sure whether the killer is trying to put one over on him, to feign contrition while trying to manipulate him into lending him a few more moments of fame. "He's obviously a sociopath and a narcissist," Gibson says. "He could be gaming us all. How can you tell about shit like that?"

For his purposes, it doesn't matter. It's what the killer did that matters to Greg Gibson, not why.

My purposes are a little less clear-cut.

Like Gibson, I too had developed a deep suspicion of the stories people tell me. Decades spent as a crime reporter, talking with all species of criminals—thieves, rapists, child molesters, killers—taught me to be on the lookout for telltale signs that could help me gauge the veracity of a tale. A sudden change in tense in a story told about a horror, abruptly switching from the detached distance of the past tense to the in-the-moment-this-is-happening-right-now urgency of the present tense, is often a good indicator that the storyteller is not only telling the truth about what they witnessed or did, but that they're reliving it right there in front of you.

It's a common phenomenon, psychologists say. You can test it for yourself, if you're heartless enough, by asking a combat veteran or a survivor of a mass shooting to recount in detail the moments of their trauma.

Conversely, parsing words to minimize responsibility or a change in voice, from the active to the passive, from "I did this" to "and then this happened," can often be a signal that a criminal's claims of contrition for their deeds warrant further scrutiny.

I've seen those two latter phenomena play out throughout my career, but never as overtly as I have while researching this book.

Take, for example, the once-upon-a-time teenage girl, now a woman in late middle age, who opened fire from her living room window onto a schoolyard full of children and adults in the 1979 mass shooting later immortalized in the catchy Top 40 hit "I Don't Like Mondays." At her last parole hearing in 2016, after four decades in a

California women's prison, she answered almost every question directly, acknowledging that she had a history of delinquent behavior, a drug and alcohol addiction, that she had been diagnosed as a threat to herself and others, that she had been repeatedly raped by her father, the last time less than two days before the shooting. Though in that latter instance, the killer had a legitimate claim to the mantle of victimhood, she told the parole board that she took full responsibility for everything she did that day. Everything except for the actual murders themselves. Those were unintentional, she maintained, an accidental consequence of her attempt to commit suicide by cop. Though she was, by her own account, a decent shot with the .22 rifle fitted with a scope her father had bought her for Christmas when what she really wanted was a radio, she insisted that she "wasn't using the sights, or aiming or anything" when she fired thirty-six rounds and placed eleven of them on her targets, killing two and injuring nine on that bleak Monday morning in January.[5]

Her parole application was denied.

Or take the account of one of the two Jonesboro shooters, the boys mocked by the killer from Columbine as "those fucks . . . with camouflage and .22s" who killed five and wounded ten when they pulled a fire alarm at their middle school and opened fire on their classmates as they poured out of the door on March 24, 1984. The Columbine killer had been right about the camouflage. He had been wrong about the rifles. The older of the Jonesboro shooters was carrying a "thirty-aught-six with a telescopic scope," and the two killers had brought at least nine other weapons with them.

The only school killers ever to be released from custody—because of their very young ages, thirteen and eleven, they were charged as juveniles and released when they turned eighteen—they were named as defendants in a successful civil suit and were ordered to give depositions years after the massacre.

In his deposition the older of the two takes the passive-voice gambit to a level I had never heard before. He too insists that he had never actually aimed at anybody when he fired his first shot. He then goes way beyond "this happened" and instead seems to blame his borrowed rifle and handguns for the slayings, as if the weapons had acted on their own, as if he were as shocked by it all as everyone else.

"My thirty-aught-six, you know, it hit Ms. Wright," he testified calmly, referring to his thirty-two-year-old teacher, Shannon Wright, whom he had gunned down from his perch two football fields away. She "got killed, very unfortunately, and one or two other people got hit with two bullets. Two of my bullets hit three people."[6]

Both a family member and a guy who'd shared an apartment with the killer around the time he gave his deposition—they spoke on condition that I not name them and not quote them directly—assured me that I was not reading too much into his sentence structure. The killer, they said, had never fully accepted responsibility for his deeds.

Nor had either of the killers given up on their fascination with guns.

Though he never again got into trouble with the law, the younger of the two attracted national attention nonetheless after the *Arkansas Times* reported in 2008 that he had applied for and been denied a concealed-carry permit. He was killed in a car crash in 2019.[7]

The older of the two killers, who did end up serving a brief federal sentence later on unrelated charges, also kept at least one firearm around during the time he gave his deposition, his temporary roommate told me.

He claimed he needed it for protection against people who might want to victimize him, the roommate said, adding that during that period he tended to sleep with one eye open, worried about what the killer's gun might do next.

All of that, my years of experience, my research, makes me hypervigilant as I begin my series of discussions with the Simon's Rock murderer. I'm examining his every word, looking for subtle clues that might tell me whether he is being truthful or toying with me.

I can tell you in advance that not once in any of our discussions does he drift into the present tense. On the other hand, he never slips into the passive voice either.

He's in his mid-forties now, and this killer, who went from Taiwan to Billings, Montana, to Simon's Rock College in the western woods of Massachusetts, has picked up a very slight hint of a New England accent after nearly thirty years in a Bay State prison. It's so slight I don't even notice it until he brings it up in answer to a question about his upbringing. "I don't really have an accent," he tells me. "If anything, I've maybe picked up more of a Boston accent than anything else."

"I've been here so long," he says, adding that he's never lived anywhere longer than he's lived at the Massachusetts Correctional Institution–Cedar Junction.

It makes me wonder whether it's just an innocent aside or if this murderer—who claims to have had such a hard time fitting in with the precocious, flamboyantly eccentric kids at Simon's Rock, a high school for ultrabright, often creative students ready for a college experience—is now trying to subtly persuade me that he has at last learned to adapt to his environment.

On paper, at least, he was not all that different from the other kids at Simon's Rock when he started there at seventeen, he tells me. He had earned respectable grades at the Catholic high school he had attended in Billings, he says, at least up until the second semester of his sophomore year, when his grades and his mood began to sour.

JOKERS WILD

He was as accomplished in the softer arts as one could be expected to be at that age. He was a decent enough violin player. He had started playing at the age of four. During his first, two-year sojourn in the United States when he was about seven, he not only became proficient at English, he also proved adroit enough to earn a chair in the local youth orchestra, he tells me. Later, after returning to the United States and while in high school, he attended the Aspen Music Festival and School, where he further sharpened his skills. It was the spring following that summer away from home that the murderer, raised by a strict immigrant father and a hard-working mom and chafing under their watch, made an effort to break free of them.

That February, he tells me, the school band and some other young musicians from Billings took a drive out to Seattle for a regional music festival, and while there, he took a liking to a girl from Oregon. When Easter break came along, the high school sophomore stole his mother's car and drove out to see her. He casts it now as "typical teenage rebellious stuff that I got myself into." And to be sure, if you were to scour the records of high school students anywhere as closely as we now scour the murderer's, you'd probably find a few others who have illicitly taken their mother's grocery-getter on a lovestruck joyride. A couple of them might even have attended Simon's Rock over the years.

The sparse paper record, of course, doesn't tell the whole story. It doesn't reveal, for instance, that at least one of his teachers, a lay Franciscan who also served as his guidance counselor, noted a steady decline in the murderer's emotional state. As Greg Gibson notes in his book, that counselor became worried enough about the stress the murderer was under from his demanding father, a former Taiwanese military man, and his mother that he fretted that the murderer might someday consider suicide. The counselor even went so far as to raise the issue with his higher-ups. They did not pursue it. The paper record addresses none of that.

Neither does the murderer.

"It was a good place," the murderer tells me of his time in Billings. "I enjoyed my time there. And my family's been there ever since. They feel that they found a home there. And I still consider that my home."

It was as good a place as any to sponge up the ambient sounds of the heartbeat of the American heartland, to immerse himself in popular culture. And he did it with as much gusto as any kid, he tells me, though his tastes ran to the darker side.

By the time he was in his teens, the once-promising violinist had become a big fan of hardcore music. He found other routes to assimilation outside the music world, he says. The 1984 flick *Red Dawn*, for example, really hit home for him—his adopted home, anyway.

"I grew up on that movie," he tells me. It's a testosterone-soaked shoot-'em-up aimed directly at teenage boys, set in the great American West during some imagined World War III, starring the late Patrick Swayze and Charlie Sheen as two brothers who gather a posse of other boys and every small arm that they can get their hands on and single-handedly take on the brutal invaders. It was a shot right to the heart of middle-American teenage boys, a flag-waving, over-the-top melodrama, bristling with perfidious enemies and overladen with heroic young men standing up to their oppressors with nothing but their courage and their God-given right to bear arms. In truth it was every shoot-'em-up ever made, just wrapped in the flag and laced with a dose of anything-goes-after-Armageddon abandon, and it's hardly surprising that it would find an avid fan in a teen from Taiwan trying hard to be an American in America's heartland.

Indeed, as the killer edged closer to leaving Billings for

the lush woods of Great Barrington, Massachusetts, he had also begun to adopt a darker, more archly right-wing pose, one laced liberally with a dose of doom.

It did not serve him well among his liberal schoolmates at Simon's Rock, he tells me. He didn't need to. Thalheimer had already laid all that out for me. "He was kind of weird," she says, "but we were all . . . weird kids."

"This was like 1992, so most of the weird kids were like *alternative*. Think like industrial-music alternative kinds of kids. People who were smart but . . . didn't fit in in their regular school," she says. The soon-to-be killer, however, was weird on an entirely different level. His music was different—"He was into hardcore," she says— and his hair was different, in that unlike many of her friends, his wasn't spray-painted purple. And he did have an alarming tendency to just sort of glower at people as if they were the advance guard of an invading Soviet Army moving across the frozen western plains and he was Patrick Swayze.

But nobody took it too seriously. He was just one weird kid in a sea of weird kids.

And while he didn't find a warm embrace in the student body at Simon's Rock, he wasn't entirely friendless, either.

He had a small clique of like-minded friends—or so they thought—with whom he'd sit at a table in the dining hall, making dark and sometimes disturbing comments just loud enough for the people at the next few tables to hear. His friends all knew it was an act, a pose, and they treated the whole thing as a kind of inside joke.

They just naturally assumed that the killer was in on it too.

So did the rest of the student body, Thalheimer says. "He and a group of friends sat at the same table at the dining hall and were not super friendly. But I don't think people looked at him and thought 'murderous intent.' You know, just like, he's a little hardcore, I'm just not going to hang with him."

They didn't know the half of it.

As his first year at Simon's Rock slipped into his second, he embraced an in-your-face, far-right persona, and he took it to extreme limits, denying the Holocaust, for example, or arguing in a class paper that gay people ought to be segregated from society to stem the spread of HIV. Somewhere along the line he melded his delight with the paranoid me-against-the-world *Red Dawn* antics with an interest in the gory writings of an ancient hermit on a Greek island somewhere who summoned visions of pale horses and pale riders and apocalyptic ruin. At his trial his defense lawyers would say that he started hearing voices. He now denies that.

"I never *heard* voices," he says. "It was more of a feeling. It wasn't even an urge. It was just a feeling. It's very hard to describe. It wasn't an urge that was telling me to kill people. It was an urge to read the book of Revelation in the Bible. I think after that, the urges . . . came from myself."

There was no single triggering event, no sudden crisis in his life. Though he "wasn't getting along with the kids at Simon's Rock," he tells me, there was no particular insult or egregious slight that sparked his rampage. The buildup to the rampage was long and slow, methodical, and it was, he says, surprisingly unencumbered by anything in the world outside his head. "I think the idea came first—because I was getting close to my birthday, my eighteenth birthday," he says, the age at which he would be legally entitled to stroll into a rifle shop in Great Barrington, flash his Montana driver's license, and purchase a Chinese knockoff of the Russia-made SKS, a very *Red Dawn*–looking semiautomatic rifle that he had been eyeing in newspaper ads.

And as he waited for his eighteenth birthday to arrive,

he purchased a large amount of ammunition, ordering it by mail and having it shipped to his dorm. He was amazed at how easy it was. The school became aware of the shipment but accepted the murderer's explanation that the box contained gun parts he had ordered as a gift for his father, and they didn't press it. They took his word for it because that's the sort of thing one does at a liberal arts college in the woods of western Massachusetts. It was the first of a series of missteps and missed cues that continued right up to the night of the slayings. In his book, Greg Gibson sees those missteps as failures that contributed to the murders. Others touched by the murders are more forgiving, and they willingly accept the college's defense of its inaction. "Hindsight is 20/20," Thalheimer tells me. "But . . . this is 1992 . . . before this became the epidemic that it is today."

If Gibson sees the utter lack of impediments—not just those at the school but on the streets of Great Barrington and in the faraway warehouse of a mail-order ammunition dealer—as failures, the killer took them as a sign that God or St. John of Patmos or Patrick Swayze or some bizarre amalgamation of them all had smiled on his plot. Or at least that's what he tells me.

"There were many instances along the way that convinced me of this," he tells me. "The fact that I was able to so easily order ammunition via the company when just weeks earlier, I had tried to order a calculator through this electronics store in New York, and they called the cops because they thought I stole someone's credit card."

"Another instance was . . . there was this little magazine stand, a little magazine kiosk in the town of Great Barrington, and my friends and I used to go in there. I would pick up the *Penthouse*s or the *Playboy*s. There was an old lady in there and I guess I looked much younger than everybody else and the old lady would always be,

'Young man, I don't think you're old enough to read that.' Of course, when I walked into the gun store, nobody ever said that to me. I couldn't get a magazine, but here I am able to get a gun."

There was no bright red line he crossed as he moved through what experts tell us are the usual stages that lead to a mass public shooting.

He went from a vague and gathering rage, amplified by a narcissistic image of himself as some kind of hero out of a video, to predator. He took the steps Meloy has identified in his work, from fixation to identification to killer.

He had carefully and methodically prepared for the killings, ordering the ammunition, trying to conceal it, purchasing the gun—as many of these killers do, just in time to commit the slaying. He threw out signals of his intent; "leakage" is the word the experts use to describe it.

And there were a half-dozen points along the line where he could have been stopped.

If the school had been able to suss out the very real menace behind his disturbing writings and his scowling countenance when even his friends at the dining hall table couldn't see through the mask . . .

If the school had been more aggressive in examining the box of bullets he got through the mail . . .

If the mail-order ammunition dealer had been as rigorous in its processes as an electronics store in Manhattan had been . . .

"If I hadn't been able to buy a gun that morning . . . ," the killer tells me.

After all that, after all those failures, was there anything that could have stopped the murderer other than the malfunction of his own rifle?

"Would a good guy with a gun have stopped you?" I ask.

He weighs his words carefully. He tells me emphatically that he is not offering this as an excuse for his crimes. He doesn't flinch at the word "murder," and when he uses it in a sentence, it's in the first person. The only thing he blames his gun for is misfiring. In fact, he doesn't even blame the gun for that. That was all him and his botched attempt to make the weapon more deadly.

He is a murderer, he says, and he is responsible for what he did that evening, twenty years to the day before the murders at Sandy Hook. He counts himself lucky, he says, that he's still alive to recount the atrocity he committed. "Often I talk about how lucky I am that I've even been given a second chance at life because in many states, twenty-five years after the fact, I probably would have been executed for what I've done."

Months later he sends me a message through Greg Gibson to underscore that thought. He tells me that he's simply trying to point out how pervasive the image of the lone, armed man standing up against his oppressors is in our culture and how, under the right circumstances, or the wrong ones, it can give solace and cover to a killer.

"Would a good guy with a gun have stopped you?" I had asked.

"I thought I was the good guy with the gun," he says.

There's one of those long deep silences over the phone. And then we fill it.

He tells me that he's had a lot of time in prison to reflect on his crimes, with a lot more ahead of him—he's serving two life sentences with no chance of ever being paroled. He says he's grateful that Greg Gibson has given him the chance to use himself as a kind of cautionary tale, to help build support for initiatives that might help stem gun violence.

He tells me that he's haunted by the thought that the massacre at Sandy Hook might have been inspired by his crimes exactly twenty years earlier, though there's no more evidence that the Sandy Hook killer took any notice of him than there is that the Virginia Tech slayer was inspired by him. "When Newtown happened, it . . . really scared me," he says. "Newtown is only, what? Sixty, seventy miles from Simon's Rock?

"So when it happened on the same exact day—I don't say this because I'm narcissistic and thinking, 'Oh, there has to be some connection'—but obviously there could have been. And it would have killed me if it did."

He seems sincere.

Seems.

"These indeed 'seem,' for they are actions that a man might play," Shakespeare's original mass killer warns us.

As I hang up the phone, I wonder: Is this killer gaming me? This "sociopath and . . . narcissist," as Gibson describes him, whose barely perceptible hint of a Boston accent is so slight that you only notice it when he calls your attention to it? Has he sussed out the arc of my narrative, and has he teased out in our conversations a sense of what he thinks I want to hear? Is he now parroting my thoughts—or Greg Gibson's—back to me in the hope that he'll receive a few more drops of ink in exchange for saying the "right" things about the blood he spilled?

Or is he honestly trying to offer me some insight into the nature of one public shooter in the sincere hope that we might be able to use that information to help thwart the next killer?

Or is it a little bit of both?

I have no idea.

Neither does Greg Gibson.

And neither do you.

And that is a big part of our problem.

Chapter 6

If You See Something, Say Something

T HE SILENCE BETWEEN gunshots was deafening, and the cops taking cover where they could find it at the bottom of the stairway tried to fill it, almost pleading with the boy to throw down his weapons and come out.

The echoes of gunshots, rounds fired by the boy, rounds fired in return from the cops, still rang in the hallways of the hundred-year-old school. Smoke and the stench of spent powder hung in the air. It had happened so fast. It hadn't even been ten minutes since the central dispatch in Richmond, Indiana, had gotten a frantic phone call from the boy's mother, telling them that her troubled son had armed himself with a .45-caliber handgun and a Remington 700, just like the one the killer in Austin had used decades earlier, that he had taken her boyfriend hostage and had ordered him at gunpoint to drive him to the Dennis Intermediate School.

It's not that there hadn't been warning signs. Counselors had warned her that her son was dangerous, that he heard voices and was possibly suicidal, potentially even homicidal, that he had expressed a desire to go to his old school and take revenge on classmates who he believed had bullied him. Seven months before he stormed into his old school, he had been held under psychiatric observation for ten days, but his mother took him out when her insurance ran out. She'd later be called to account for that decision. In October 2019 authorities charged her with a raft of offenses—five felony counts of neglect of a dependent, one felony count of dangerous control of a child, and one misdemeanor count of criminal recklessness—for failing to prevent her son from storming into his own school with the intent to commit murder.[1] But on that day in December she told authorities that she couldn't believe that he intended to hurt anyone, no one other than himself, at least. The two hundred rounds of .223 ammunition he carried with him for the rifle, the fifty or so shells for the pistol, and the Molotov cocktails he had fashioned out of old water bottles and rags told a different story. As did the detailed plan for the attack that he had written around the time he posed for pictures with his weapons and posted them on social media.

The boy had planned to do "maximum damage," police would later say. Later, perhaps, investigators would have the luxury of time to parse the clues the boy had left, the signals he had sent, the warning signs that were missed or misunderstood. Later there would be time to wonder whether the nearly friendless boy who had never really been able to fit into the school—he was now being schooled at home—could have been identified as a risk to himself or others earlier.

But not now.

Now there was only one objective: to neutralize the boy with the guns before he could unleash havoc on the roughly 650 fifth- through eighth-graders and their teachers at the school. With luck they could take the kid alive.

Whatever clues and warning signs might have been missed in the days leading up to the planned rampage at Dennis Intermediate School, the grim lessons of school shootings past had been learned, and the cops in that hallway knew that every second counted. Even the dispatchers had learned that lesson. Several weeks earlier the lead investigator from the Sandy Hook mass shooting had visited Indiana to teach first responders the proper protocol for an active-shooter situation. He told them that they needed to throw the careful, calming scripts that they had been taught to use in most emergencies out the window when a report came in about a potential active shooter. In such situations, he told them, every second is worth up to three lives, and every second wasted on an extraneous question could mean the difference between life and death for somebody. What difference does it make how many wounded there are, he asked them, when the first cops on the scene are going to choke back their own human instinct for compassion and step right over them to get to the killer, to stop the killing before they stop the dying? "It's all about shaving seconds," he told them.

And they had listened. The frantic mother wasn't even off the phone when the dispatcher notified the school, and the school went on lockdown and broadcast a "be on the lookout" for the boy and his hostage driver. The kid and the first two cops had arrived at the school almost simultaneously. They had been right behind him when he fired three rounds from the .45 to blast out the window on the front door. They had been just steps behind him when he had tugged on those classroom doors, identifying himself as a police officer demanding to be let inside.

His childish voice—straining to sound like a

man's—hadn't fooled anybody. He was only fourteen, after all. It had taken just minutes from the moment the mom's call came in, but the staff and teachers were ready for him—as ready as one can ever be when the it-can't-happen-here happens here. And as he dashed down the hall and up the stairwell, taking cover behind a fire door, the school's principal had watched his every move on the school's video security system, relaying his movements to police dispatchers who in turn warned the cops where the danger lurked.

Other cops arrived quickly, and the boy with the guns showed no sign that he was ready to surrender. He fired two more rounds from the .45, through the door and through the little glass window in it; when the pistol was empty he picked up the Remington, and over the next few moments let seven more rounds fly. The cops returned fire. "We were not having any more luck hitting him than he was hitting our guys," Police Chief Jim Branum told me. Not that they wanted to. They knew this was a kid, a kid with two guns and a cache of ammunition, but a kid nonetheless. And they spoke to him as if he was a child. "Give it up, buddy," one cop said. "This isn't going to work." There was a gentleness in his voice. There was none of that "typical cop-speak," Branum said, "none of that, 'Put down the gun, asshole,' stuff." It was an order, yes. But it was also a plea. And it hung for a moment in the silence between gunshots.

"Give me a second," the kid finally replied. "I'm reloading."

A moment later, a single gunshot rang out. Just as his mother had feared, the kid had taken his own life.

In the grand scheme of things in America today, what happened that day in Richmond, Indiana, was a successful police operation, Branum said. The cops responded professionally and courageously and several lives were no doubt saved. But one young life was lost. And there isn't a cop who was in the hallway that day who doesn't wonder whether that one lost kid could have been saved.

A half century of horror has taught us some hard lessons, the cops and the analysts who study mass public shootings will tell you.

We've learned the hardest way possible that every tick of the clock matters when a killer bent on killing more than the last killer is on the loose. We've learned that in those chaotic moments when a mass shooting is underway, our human instincts toward compassion and kindness must sometimes be ignored, that sometimes you have to step over the wounded to save lives, that you have to stop the killing before you can stop the dying.

But we're still struggling with the hardest lesson: the challenge of trying to determine who among us is likely to become the next mass killer. In popular culture we've created myths that give us the false comfort of thinking that we can spot them in a crowd simply by their appearance. When I began this project I tried an informal little experiment. I asked almost everyone I ran into to describe a mass public shooter for me. I was stunned by how similar the answers were. In almost every case, they described a young, white male. Sometimes they gave me a romanticized Hollywood image—think the heavily armed, trench coat–clad Keanu Reeves in *The Matrix*—and sometimes it was a wild-eyed weakling like the Sandy Hook shooter, but in every case the descriptions were of young, white males. It's interesting that even the middle-aged Asian immigrant spending his life in a Massachusetts prison for a multiple murder he committed at his school a quarter century ago conjured a similar image of a mass public shooter when I posed the question to him, though he did acknowledge that he did not precisely fit the profile in the public imagination.

But the reality is, the experts who develop the tools to assess such risks tell me, that's a myth. We cannot simply profile our way out of this epidemic of mass violence based on some mistaken idea about who these killers are or what they look like. Indeed, the myth that we can identify potential mass public shooters simply by their age or by the color of their skin is not just wrong, it may be counterproductive. As one analyst told me, it runs the risk of "preventing people from seeing what they should see."

The hard truth, the experts will tell you, is that there is no single profile of a mass public shooter.

In fact, after studying 63 shooters (among a sample drawn from 160 active shooting incidents between 2000 and 2013 in the United States), the FBI concluded that—contrary to the popular idea that these shooters are disproportionately disgruntled white males in their teens and twenties—there is no single demographic from which they come.[2]

Yes, the vast majority of them are male, according to the FBI's findings. But then again, so are most of the gun owners in the United States. About 62 percent of the gun owners in America are men, according to a 2017 Pew Research Center survey, and those men are significantly more likely than women to keep their guns loaded and handy.[3]

And yes, a majority of the active shooters the FBI studied were white—63 percent of them identified as Caucasian, the FBI found.

But so are the majority of American gun owners, who never commit a crime of any description. According to a Pew Research Center survey conducted in 2017, about 30 percent of Americans say they own a gun themselves, and another 11 percent live in a household where someone else does. That 41 percent includes nearly half the white males in America. In comparison, about a third of African American households and 21 percent of Hispanic households have guns.

The upshot is, once you adjust for the rates of gun

ownership—and it's worth noting that 86 percent of the time, mass shooters acquire their weapons legally or borrow them from their legal owners[4]—the ethnic makeup of mass shooters begins to look very much like the population at large.

In the 2018 study in which the FBI narrowed the focus to sixty-three active shooters, 63 percent of them were white, 10 percent were Asian, 16 percent were African American, 6 percent identified as Hispanic, 3 percent were of Middle Eastern descent, and 2 percent were Native American.[5] That has remained fairly constant.

In other words, as one researcher who has spent decades studying mass public shooters put it to me, "People think of shooters as being white. . . . They're not. They're actually relatively in proportion, race proportion, to this country."

Nor is age necessarily a determining factor. While school shooters, for example, tend to be young, like the would-be killer at Dennis Intermediate School (one school shooter was twelve years old), those who commit workplace shootings and other kinds of mass killings tend to be older. But that, say the analysts behind the FBI study, may have more to do with the fact that these killers and would-be killers choose targets that are familiar to them and where they feel some grievance against them was committed.

On balance, however, there is no age at which this kind of atrocity is most likely to be committed. Of the shooters studied, 13 percent were under the age of eighteen, 25 percent were eighteen to twenty-nine, and almost 30 percent were in their forties, like the Tree of Life killer in Pittsburgh. Nearly a quarter of them were eligible for AARP cards. The oldest killer in the cohort the FBI studied was eighty-eight years old.

Nor was a prior diagnosis of mental illness a telltale sign. To be sure, the kid in the hallway in Richmond,

Indiana, had shown signs of severe mental illness, and perhaps, if those warnings had been heeded by those closest to him, he might have been stopped well before he took his own life. But of the sixty-three shooters studied in an FBI report, only a quarter had any documented history of a prior diagnosis for mental illness, a percentage roughly in line with the population at large, and of those sixty-three studied, only three had been diagnosed with a psychotic disorder. As noted earlier, other studies, like the multiyear analysis that *Mother Jones* conducted, found that the number was higher, though in many of those cases the illnesses were not detected until after the fact.

As the FBI's 2018 report concluded, "These 63 active shooters did not appear to be uniform in any way such that they could be readily identified prior to attacking based on demographics alone."

What they did have in common, however, were behavioral traits. And studying those behaviors, developing risk-assessment strategies based on the types of behaviors common to mass shooters, may be the best hope for catching potential mass shooters before they claim their first life, the analysts say.

There is a persistent idea that mass public shooters, and school shooters in particular, are often the victims of bullying, and some evidence backs that notion: a 2019 US Secret Service study of forty-one incidents of school violence from 2008 to 2017 found that more than 50 percent of the attackers appear to have been either bullied regularly or at least felt they had been, and in 46 percent of the cases that bullying was viewed as one precipitating factor in the attacks.[6] But as both the Secret Service study and the FBI report found, in a significant number of cases, the attackers were also likely to be bullies themselves. About a third of the attackers in the Secret Service sample had been accused of bullying. In fact, in terms of developing a risk-assessment strategy, abusive or threatening behavior—especially against women—may be one of the brightest red flags.

"We found evidence that 62 percent . . . of the active shooters had a history of acting in an abusive, harassing, or oppressive way (e.g., excessive bullying, workplace intimidation)," the 2018 FBI report stated.

In a significant number of cases, that intimidating behavior was directed at women. At least "16 percent had engaged in intimate partner violence; and 11 percent had engaged in stalking-related conduct," the FBI researchers concluded, adding that because incidents of domestic violence and stalking tend to be underreported, that number may be far higher.

In other words, mass killers and would-be mass killers often send out a number of warning signs days, weeks, months—sometimes even years—before their attacks. But often those warning signs are missed, ignored, or downplayed, analysts say.

Take the August 2019 case in the small Ohio burg of New Middletown, where a would-be shooter was arrested and charged with making threats against the nearby Youngstown Jewish Family Center. Though media reports of the arrest focused largely on his public posturing as a white supremacist—the twenty-year-old, who sometimes dressed as an IRA member, had attended the 2017 Unite the Right rally of white supremacists in Charlottesville, Virginia, and had posted racist and anti-Semitic comments on social media—he also had a history of alarming behavior toward women, Police Chief Vince D'Egidio said.

In fact, it was that behavior that brought the young man to the attention of the police.

Though the young man had no criminal record—"We had no history with him," D'Egidio told me, "except some minor criminal mischief . . . juvenile versus juvenile stuff when he was younger"—the cops had been aware of him.

In a small Ohio town, a guy parading around the streets in the borrowed costume of an Irish Republican Army terrorist, spouting racist propaganda on the Internet, kind of stands out, D'Egidio said. "We always had our eye on him because he was always going around wearing like a black jacket that said IRA on it, things of that nature. So that always raised some red flags for us."

But it wasn't until they got a complaint from a young woman that he had allegedly harassed—a complaint that surfaced just days after a string of mass shootings in Gilroy, California; El Paso, Texas; and across the state in Dayton—that authorities launched a full-scale investigation. The woman told them that she had received troubling messages from the wannabe IRA terrorist. More than that, he had been harassing her, and in recent days he had keyed her car, she said. As investigators probed deeper, they found even more troubling allegations, D'Egidio said. Among them was a claim that several years ago, while still in high school, "he was pursuing a young lady . . . and to impress her, he burned a squirrel alive and sent her that."

It took the increased vigilance born in the wake of three highly publicized mass shootings to bring those allegations to light, but the police moved quickly, and within five and a half hours of their first encounter with the female target of the suspected shooter's obsession, they had him in custody and had amassed enough evidence to charge him with telephone harassment and aggravated menacing, the chief said. They also seized a cache of weapons from his home, including two AR-15 rifles and dozens of rounds of .223 ammunition for them, as well as other firearms. Also confiscated were a gas mask and a bulletproof vest, both critical elements of the costume worn by several mass public shooters in the past.

That same week in August 2019, police in two other American communities arrested young men who they believed were plotting atrocities. In Daytona Beach, Florida, for example, police got a tip that indicated that a disturbed young man was planning a mass shooting, again from a woman who was enduring unwanted advances from him. In that case, the young man had tried to enlist the young woman as an accomplice. According to a police report filed by the Volusia County Sheriff's Department, the young man had not only demonstrated an obsession with mass shooters of the past, a common trait among many shooters, he had also expressed a desire to outdo them in terms of the carnage he hoped to wreak—to, in effect, kill the last killer. "A good 100 kills would be nice," he wrote to her in one missive. "I already have a location," he added, decorating his message with a laughing face emoji. "Is that bad?"

There is, perhaps, an insight into the mind of that particular suspect in one almost plaintive line he wrote her. "Was kinda hoping someone would come into my life worth not doing it for, for the sake of all those people," he wrote, again decorating the message with the laughing emoji.[7]

Though they are not always as graphic and overt, preattack warnings are common enough among potential mass public shooters that experts and analysts have coined a word for them. They call the warnings "leakage." According to the 2018 FBI study, in more than half of the cases studied (56 percent) the shooters at least hinted at their intentions—leaked—either publicly or directly to someone they knew. Among shooters under the age of eighteen, the number was even higher—88 percent. It's important to note that the leaked threats are not always specific, nor do they necessarily identify a specific target.

"The leaked intent to commit violence was not always directed at the eventual victims of the shootings; in some cases what was communicated was a more general goal of doing harm to others, apparently without a particular person or group in mind. For example, one active shooter talked to a clerk at a gas station about killing 'a family' and another expressed interest in becoming a sniper like a character featured in *The Turner Diaries*," the report stated.

Nor is the threat always directed at another. Nearly half the killers studied had at least entertained the thought of committing suicide in the twelve months before they committed their atrocities, and a quarter of them had made a suicide attempt. It's critical to understand, the report notes, that recognizing that mass killers often harbor suicidal thoughts is not an indictment of those who are suffering from mental illness and depression who also entertain thoughts of taking their own lives. Rather, it presents an opportunity to save even more lives than those that would be taken by a mass killer:

> The high levels of pre-attack suicidal ideation—with many appearing within 12 months of the attack—are noteworthy as they represent an opportunity for intervention. If suicidal ideation or attempts in particular are observed by others, reframing bystander awareness within the context of a mass casualty event may help to emphasize the importance of telling an authority figure and getting help for the suicidal person. Without stigmatizing those who struggle with thoughts of self-harm, researchers and practitioners must continue to explore those active shooters who combined suicide with externalized aggression (including homicidal violence) and identify the concurrent behaviors that reflect this shift.[8]

And yet, at least in those sixty-three cases studied in the 2018 report, warning signs were often ignored, or, as in the case of the kid in the hallway in Richmond, Indiana, not brought to the attention of law enforcement until it was too late. Indeed, in many cases multiple warning signs were ignored or underplayed, the study found. On average, active shooters displayed five separate, identifiable warning signs before launching their attacks, the study found. But in most cases those warning signs were not enough to trigger the involvement of either law enforcement or mental health authorities.

Increasingly, however, progress has been made to change that. Throughout the nation colleges and universities and businesses have begun to develop threat assessment teams, which focus not on outward appearance but on behavioral clues that may indicate who the next public mass shooter might be. But such assessments may also address a host of other issues, from emotional distress to mental health, without necessarily stigmatizing people. Because many of the same behaviors that mass public shooters exhibit—a fascination with violence, a sense of grievance, open hostility, conflicts in interpersonal interactions—are also seen in a sea of other Americans who may act out in other ways (domestic violence or suicide, for example) or who may just suffer alone and in silence. Learning to read the clues could mean that many of those people can get the help they need and reduce other forms of violence in this nation, one of the analysts behind the FBI report told me.

As D'Egidio, the police chief in New Middletown, put it, it all boils down to the hard lesson we learned after 9/11. "If you see something, say something."

CHAPTER 7

A Good Guy
with a Gun

STEPHEN WILLEFORD WASN'T really asleep, though
he knew he ought to be. He had a grueling week ahead
working the late shift as a plumber up in San Antonio,
some fifty miles from home, and even an hour or two of
shut-eye on this balmy and cloudless November Sunday
morning in 2017 would be welcome.

It was sometime after 11:30 a.m. when his daughter
came bursting through the door. "There's gunfire," she
said. Groggy and half asleep, it took him a moment to
process what she had said. He heard something, a faint
sound, and he first imagined that someone was tapping at
his bedroom window. "I opened the window, and no, there
wasn't no one there," he said.

"Come into the kitchen," his daughter ordered him.

From there he could hear it as clear as hell—the awful, mechanical jackhammer bang of a semiautomatic rifle, a sound that, as a competitive shooter, he knew far too well to mistake for anything else. Before he could gather his thoughts and make it to his gun safe, his twenty-six-year-old daughter was out the door. Unarmed, unprotected, she had dashed out to her car and raced up the street to confirm their worst nightmare. In an instant, she was back. "Some guy is shooting up the church," she said as she burst back through the door.

Later, the fear and the anger of a father whose daughter had just exposed herself to extreme danger would hit him, and Willeford would rail at her for her recklessness, her foolhardiness. It would take the intervention of an old friend gently reminding him that "her problem is that she's too much like her father" to soothe his rage. But at that moment, there was no time. He sprinted to his gun safe. Deftly dialing in the combination, he instinctively reached for his favorite AR-15, the one with a holographic sight he had scored high marks with blasting away at bowling pins in shooting competitions. He loaded it and, barefoot, raced out the front door and up the street to the First Baptist Church of Sutherland Springs, Texas, reaching the street outside just as an armor-clad gunman—who had already shot twenty-six people to death—was preparing inside to claim a twenty-seventh life, a man he had already shot once in the back.

Willeford still doesn't know what made him do it—in hindsight, he concedes, it could be considered as foolhardy as his daughter's decision to race to the church "with nothing in her hand"—but as soon as he got to the church he called out to the killer inside, giving away his position beside an old parked truck.

For reasons that Willeford still doesn't fully understand, the killer dropped his semiautomatic rifle inside the church and, armed with a handgun instead, stalked outside. It is not at all clear if the killer knew an armed citizen, a "good guy with a gun," was waiting outside for him or whether the sound of Willeford's voice alone was enough to momentarily disrupt the massacre.

The killer, clad in the stereotypical tactical vest and a helmet with a dark visor, lumbered out of the front door. "I couldn't see his face. I couldn't see anything but his lower chin," the good guy with the gun recalled. "I could have been shooting at a robot."

"He started shooting at me," Willeford said, "and I returned fire." There wasn't even time for fear to take hold, he says. "Just a hyper sense of everything. You know. He came out and he started taking shots at me, and I hit him." The rounds weren't fatal. The killer's off-the-rack Class 3 body armor was capable of withstanding a hit from a bullet traveling at more than 1,400 feet per second.

But they were enough to halt the killer in his tracks. Citing the autopsy report, the good guy with the gun notes that the killer "had a contusion on his left chest, a contusion on his abdomen. Those are my first two shots . . . but that worked. . . . He stopped shooting at me at that moment and ran for his truck. And when he turned aside I put one in his side and one in his leg."

"He got in his vehicle," Willeford said. Then, switching to the telltale present tense, he adds that the killer "shoots through the side window at me."

Less than ten minutes had passed since the shooting had begun. Even less time had passed since his daughter had roused him out of his half slumber. Now, as the killer pulled away, the good guy leveled his rifle, aiming through the car window at the spot where he expected the killer's head to be. "I pulled the trigger and they say he had an abrasion across his forehead." As the killer sped down the road, "I put one through the back window—hit the back window on the driver's side seat and hit him just right of the left shoulder blade. That was my last shot that hit him," he said.

In the chaos, a stranger, a twenty-seven-year-old from Seguin named Johnnie Langendorff who happened to be in town visiting his girlfriend, sat in his truck at a stoplight watching the shootout on the main street of this town of six hundred. "I turned around and I looked at a tall guy sitting at a stoplight," the good guy with the gun said. "I ran over. I didn't even know John, didn't know his name, never seen him before in my life. I just tapped on his window and said, 'That guy just shot up the church and we have to stop him.' And then I heard the doors unlock to his truck and I climbed in."

It was only later that it dawned on Willeford that Langendorff had figured out on his own who the good guy with the gun was that morning and who the bad guy was. "I was barefoot and the other guy had body armor on. I guess he was able to put that together in his head. And he let me into his truck. And we gave chase. We chased him over eleven miles," he said, keeping in contact with 911 the whole way.

At one point, about eight miles outside of town, the killer lost control of his Ford Explorer and ran into a ditch. The two good guys pulled up behind him. It was then that the barefoot man realized he only had two more rounds left in his magazine. But this time, the murderer didn't shoot back. Instead, he gunned the engine and took off again down the road, making it only a few hundred yards before he crashed through a fence and came to a final stop in the middle of a field. The killer called his wife. He called his father. He told them he had done a terrible thing, and that he wasn't going to make it. And then "he put the gun to his head and pulled the trigger and did us all a favor."

There was again that awful silence between gunshots,

and deep inside that silence, the barefoot man could hear a distant voice telling him that he did indeed have it in him to kill another man, if that was what was required of him. He was grateful that he did not have to. "I don't have to tell anybody that I killed anybody," he said. "Because I didn't. He did it himself."

"I don't believe we're wired by God to want to kill," he later told me. "But I would have."

The only thing that stops a bad guy with a gun is a good guy with a gun.

It is one of the most durable tales we tell ourselves in the wake of massacres like Sutherland Springs. Long before NRA executive president Wayne LaPierre glibly coined the phrase in his now-famous pronouncement a week after the 2012 murders of twenty-seven, twenty of them children killed in their classrooms, at Sandy Hook Elementary School, the notion persisted that an armed populace, locked and loaded and ready to take on a psychopathic killer, can save lives, despite the chaos and confusion of a surprise attack by a heavily armed killer. It's an epic myth we've clung to since the beginning of the American experiment: the idea of the lone hero, armed with a gun and good intentions, High Nooning it against a motivated murderer and prevailing.

It was tested in 1966 with mixed results in the very first modern mass public shooting when, as I noted in the prologue, students and other civilians raced home to fetch their hunting rifles and returned to open fire on a killer armed with a long-range rifle hundreds of feet above them in the University of Texas Tower. As author Gary Lavergne, who painstakingly researched every heartbeat of that first mass public shooting, told me, it is possible that the sporadic barrage from the ground may have saved some lives, forcing the killer to take cover behind the stone balustrade of the observation deck, perhaps limiting his ability to target innocent people and slowing his rate of fire. But it also may have impeded the ability of the heroic first responders—Austin police officers Houston McCoy and Ramiro Martinez and newly deputized civilian Allen Crum—to confront and ultimately kill the killer, he said. As Martinez later recalled, slipping into that distinctive present tense a half century after the murders, "Bullets keep coming up at us. They crack—you could hear the crack as they go over your head, and then they'd hit the Tower. Dust would come down, rain down in little particles of stone."[1]

Even after the killer lay dead that August afternoon in 1966, the shooting from the ground continued, placing the heroes who had ended the massacre in personal peril. "There are radio recordings where they're pleading with people to tell the civilians to quit shooting," Lavergne notes.

But despite its durability as a trope, the evidence that a "good guy with a gun" is a reasonable response to a body armor–clad murderer with a semiautomatic rifle or a rapid-fire handgun is, at best, inconclusive. Indeed, out of 277 active-shooter situations analyzed by the FBI in three separate studies from 2000 to 2018, unarmed civilians halted 11.19 percent of the incidents, whereas only 3.9 percent were ended by "good guys with guns."[2]

In its exhaustive study of 160 active-shooter cases between 2000 and 2013, for example, the FBI found that 56.3 percent of the time it wasn't a good guy with a gun who stopped the killing; it was the bad guy himself. Twenty-nine of those shooters fled the scene before police showed up, according to the study. Nearly a quarter of the time (23.1 percent), they killed themselves in the moments before armed police officers arrived.[3]

In twenty-one cases, however, it was "good guys *without* a gun" who brought the mayhem to an end, confronting and restraining the shooter until help arrived. It's worth noting that half of those unarmed good guys were teachers or staff members or students at schools where shootings happened.

In only five cases out of the 160 did the inarguably heroic actions of what LaPierre dubbed a "good guy with a gun" bring a shooter down, the report found. In those cases, three of the killers were shot to death, one was wounded, and one more committed suicide. In a study of forty incidents in the 2015–2016 report, six active shooters were restrained by bystanders, and in only two of those cases did the civilians use a firearm. In one of the four remaining cases, pepper spray did the trick.

In another study of fifty active-shooter situations in 2016 and 2017, the FBI found that civilians stopped eight of those shooters, and half of those civilians were unarmed.

Civilians confronted gunmen five more times in 2018; they were unarmed in three of those cases, bringing deadly attacks to an end, according to an FBI study of twenty-seven active-shooter incidents that year.[4]

The cold bureaucratic language of the reports doesn't capture the courage involved in those acts. You have to peer into their footnotes or scour the local newspapers to find that. In one case, in April 2018, a sneak attack on a Waffle House that killed four, wounded two, and left two others injured from broken glass ended when a heroic customer by the name of James Shaw Jr. grabbed the white-hot barrel of the killer's AR-15 and wrestled it away from him.[5] The killer, a diagnosed schizophrenic who was later determined by a court to be incompetent to stand trial, fled and was finally captured the following day after a massive manhunt.

A month later, in the comfortable middle-class town of Noblesville, Indiana, a thirteen-year-old would-be killer stormed into his science class at the Noblesville West Middle School and opened fire with a pair of handguns, critically wounding a fellow student and his science teacher, thirty-year-old Jason Seaman, who, despite his injuries, had the presence of mind to hurl a miniature basketball at the boy. The burly, muscular middle-school teacher then rushed the shooter, tackling him and pinning him to the ground as the rest of his students made it to safety.[6] Like the young killers in Jonesboro twenty years earlier, the shooter was too young to be charged as an adult and could be released from custody after he turns eighteen, though he may remain on probation until he is twenty-two.

And in November 2019, unarmed civilians again acted when a gunman with a well-documented history of hatred for women opened fire at a Hot Yoga franchise in Tallahassee, Florida, murdering two women and injuring four other people. Customers, including one man who was pistol-whipped in the process, rushed the gunman. By the time police arrived—three and a half minutes after the first shot had been fired—the gunman had already killed himself.[7]

Twice in 2018, incidents ended with the intervention of "good guys with guns," and in only one of the cases did the armed civilian manage to shoot the killer, according to the FBI report.

A deeper dive into the specifics of the cases is instructive.

On October 24, just three days before the mass shooting at the Tree of Life synagogue in Pittsburgh, a fifty-one-year-old white man who had unsuccessfully tried to break into a predominantly black church burst into a Kroger supermarket in the Louisville suburb of Jeffersontown, Kentucky, and gunned down two elderly African Americans, while sparing at least one white man who was in the store, allegedly telling that man that "whites don't shoot whites."[8]

As the killer tried to flee, he was confronted by an armed citizen, a man with a concealed-carry permit by the name of Dominiic Rozier who had gone to the store to buy candy for his son's birthday. The two exchanged gunfire on the street outside the supermarket. Neither man was hit, and the killer was arrested moments later. He faces federal hate crime and weapons charges and could get the death penalty if convicted.

In only one of those 2018 cases where good guys intervened was the shooter actually brought down by civilian gunfire. It happened on May 24, 2018, at Louie's Grill and Bar, a popular local watering hole in Oklahoma City. Two men, a former police officer turned security guard named Juan Carlos Nazario and Bryan Whittle, a federal employee who'd spent twenty years with the Oklahoma Air National Guard, exchanged gunfire with a gunman, a guy who had claimed on social media that he was under "hardcore demonic attack" and had just wounded three people.[9] The two men killed the shooter.

There are, of course, other risks that arise when civilians, even with the best of intentions, introduce firearms into an already chaotic and confusing active-shooter situation, say the experts who have studied such cases.

Take the May 7, 2019, attack on a STEM charter school in Highlands Ranch, Colorado, when two students opened fire on their schoolmates, wounding eight and killing a heroic senior named Kendrick Castillo who tried to restrain one of the shooters. In the chaos of the moment, a security guard—who unbeknownst to school officials was armed with a handgun—saw the barrel of a rifle sticking out from around a corner and fired. It was a sheriff's deputy he was firing at. He missed the first responder but wounded a female student. The case remains under investigation as this book goes to press. As John McDonald, executive director of security at Jefferson County Public Schools told the *Denver Post*, in such situations, absent exhaustive training and effective communication with official first responders, adding another gun to the mix can have tragic consequences. "There's no way for any-body in uniform to know who a good guy or a bad guy is," McDonald said.[10]

Indeed, in the fog of war that envelops everything at the scene of these deadly atrocities, even trained professionals, experienced cops, can sometimes make deadly errors. The November 7, 2018, mass shooting at the Borderline Bar and Grill, a popular country and western nightclub in Thousand Oaks, California (an atrocity we'll explore more deeply in chapter 9), is a case in point. In that incident a former Marine, who had seen combat in Afghanistan, armed himself with a Glock 21 semiautomatic pistol fitted with a laser sight and an extended magazine and opened fire on a crowd of mostly young people. Though police, some of them armed with semiautomatic rifles, responded quickly, they could not have responded fast enough to prevent the deaths of twelve innocent people that night. Among them was a police officer who died, authorities would later determine, from a round fired from a fellow officer's assault rifle.[11]

A single bullet had taken down the killer and ended the massacre. According to the autopsy report, it was a .45-caliber round fired from his own gun.[12]

It must be noted, says David Chipman, the twenty-five-year veteran of the Bureau of Alcohol, Tobacco, Firearms and Explosives who now serves as a consultant to the gun safety organization Giffords Courage to Fight Gun Violence, that at a time when motivated killers have comparatively easy access to deadly rapid-fire weapons and extended magazines capable of killing scores in seconds, even law enforcement professionals with the best of training, who may perform flawlessly in the face of such horror, can at best only limit the carnage. They can't stop it.

Take the mass shooting at the Garlic Festival in Gilroy, California, on July 28, 2019, when a nineteen-year-old killer carrying a WASR-10 semiautomatic rifle and at least 275 rounds of ammunition cut through a chain-link fence, entered a fairgrounds heavily patrolled by police officers, and opened fire. Police brought the killer down within a minute, firing multiple bullets into him, before he fired a final round himself, taking his own life. But that wasn't fast enough to stop him from squeezing off thirty-nine rounds, killing three people and injuring thirteen others.[13]

Just days later, on August 4, a twenty-four-year-old Ohio man obsessed with violence and stories of mass shooters past opened fire on the crowd in Dayton's restaurant district with an AM-15, a short-barreled pistol-like variant of an AR-15 that he had fitted with a hundred-round drum magazine. He killed nine and wounded seventeen, though police responded instantly.[14] "[They] had the quickest police response I can imagine," Chipman says. Within seconds of the first shot fired, the killer lay dead from police gunfire. Yet it wasn't fast enough. "In . . . seconds, this shooter had already killed nine people and wounded two dozen," he says.

For many people currently or formerly in law enforcement, people like Chipman who are schooled in tactics and steeped in the grim statistics of the epidemic of mass public shootings, there is little enthusiasm for the notion of adding more guns to these deadly and unpredictable cases. As Chipman notes, when he was doing joint training with the US Secret Service, the agency charged with protecting the life of the president of the United States, the participants were taught that in many life-threatening situations they wouldn't even have time to draw their service weapons, and instead might well be called on to hurl themselves in front of a bullet to stop it. The answer that the Secret Service has come up with, he says, is not to introduce more firearms into a volatile situation, but to limit them.

"The Secret Service knows that the only way they can protect someone is to create a dome of protection around the person so a gun can't get within shooting range," Chipman says. "That's it. There is no Secret Service plan like 'This is how we win the gunfight.' You can't let a gun in."

There is one other element of the "good guy with a gun" myth, he says, that gets far too little attention in the national debate: the element of human nature.

It's a hard thing to kill someone, even when the person you intend to kill is a mass murderer, he says. Even trained combat veterans hardened in the crucible of war are daunted by the idea. In a controversial 1947 study of American combat soldiers in World War II, *Men Against Fire: The Problem of Battle Command*, Brigadier General S. L. A. Marshall concluded that only about 15 percent of combat soldiers in the European theater actually fired their weapons in a firefight.[15] Call it God, call it nature, but whatever you call it, the forces that formed us did not make it easy for us to kill our own kind, even when our own lives or the lives of others depend on it. As Lt. Col. Dave Grossman, an author and scholar who has studied the science of killing, puts it in "The Psychological Effects of Combat": "Left to their own devices, the great majority of individual combatants throughout history appear to have been unable or unwilling to kill."[16]

Indeed, in high-profile mass public shooting incidents, there have been multiple cases in which trained police officers, professionals, have frozen, or second-guessed themselves, or held back, losing precious seconds, waiting for someone else to take the initiative, to open fire or to charge the killer.

In some cases, perhaps, it is a fear of killing. In others, it may be a fear of dying. And in still others, it may simply be that in the murderous chaos of a mass public shooting, even with years of simulated conditioning and training, no one knows for certain how they will react until the bullets start flying.

In what has become the most infamous such case, seven criminal charges of felony neglect of a child were filed against a Broward County deputy sheriff, Scot Peterson, alleging that he failed to act to prevent a gunman with an AR-15 from shooting thirty-four students and adults during the February 14, 2018, mass public shooting at Marjory Stoneman Douglas High School in Parkland, Florida. As the commission empaneled by the state to investigate the killings put it in their blistering analysis of Peterson's actions that day: "Peterson was derelict in his duty [and] . . . failed to act consistently with his training and fled to a position of personal safety while [the murderer] shot and killed MSDHS students and staff. Peterson was in a position to engage [the killer] and mitigate further harm to others, and he willfully decided not to do so."[17]

For his part, Peterson has denied the allegations and bristles at charges that his actions—or inaction— amounted to cowardice. It will be up to a jury to decide whether the commission's version of events or Peterson's prevails.

But the case underscores a key point that Chipman and others who study these events make: until you're tested under fire, you have no idea how you're going to react.

And even if you do have the training, skill, and presence of mind to exchange fire with a motivated murderer, even if you are one of the rare "good guys with guns" who manages to gun down a mass shooter, there will still be a debt to be paid psychologically.

Police forces have long been aware of the psychological stress the trauma of a shooting can place on officers, even when the shooting is perfectly justified. Those officers are routinely placed at least temporarily on desk duty and are offered counseling and other services. Still, if you can get a cop who has been involved with one of those shootings to open up to you—a difficult task when you're talking to a member of a profession that prides itself on stoic silence—you might get them to admit that they are haunted by the trauma of it.

Here's one example. A few years back, author Lavergne visited with Houston McCoy, a member of the heroic trio who braved gunfire from above and below to finally end the bloodshed in 1966 at the University of Texas. The visit came just a short time before the retired hero cop passed away, Lavergne said, and it was a chance to put a final coda on the record. "I asked him what he wanted people to remember about that incident," Lavergne told me. The famously taciturn cowboy cop didn't miss a beat, and in his final statement on the matter, he revealed how deeply he had been affected by what he had been called on to do that day.

"That son of a bitch made me kill a man," he said.

It takes a unique form of character to find within yourself not only the will to face a killer but the ability to marshal skill and to prevail in that kind of horrific encounter. It takes an even more unique character to find solace and comfort afterward.

You can't buy character off a rack at a sporting goods store so long as you can pass a background check—or at a gun show without one. Heroism doesn't come from the barrel of a gun. It has to be deeply imprinted in your DNA before you ever pick up the gun.

If you ask Stephen Willeford, the good guy with the gun who is justly regarded as the hero of the Sutherland Springs massacre, he'll tell you in that level, soft-spoken, small-town Texas drawl of his that even if he had no rifle, no gun at all, he would have done the same thing he did that day in November 2017. He would still have rushed toward the sound of gunfire, and he still would have called the killer out. "I would have," the fourth-generation citizen of Sutherland Springs says. "I would have. . . . I've never been a guy to stand by and let something happen to someone who's innocent. I can't do it. It's not in my nature. I can't do it."

What made him face off against that killer wasn't any stamped and pressed courage borrowed from a mass-produced rifle. It was, he says, an act of both faith and "love."

"I didn't shoot that man out of hatred for him. I shot him out of love for everybody in that church," he says, adding that "I tell people that I am a Christian, and if I had lost that fight and he would have killed me that day I would have woke up in the arms of Jesus, and that ain't a bad day either."

Indeed, he believes with perfect faith that the Almighty guided him that day, and that it wasn't he who intervened and disrupted one of the most atrocious killings in recent American history. Rather, he was simply the vessel for divine intervention. "I truly believe that God was whispering in my ear that day. And when I saw those shots fired at me, I heard in the back of my head, 'Don't worry about those shots, just do what I sent you here to do.'"

That's a rare kind of courage and faith and conviction. It's the courage of a good guy who would be a good guy whether he held a gun or not. In our culture we flatter ourselves that we all share that distinctive trait. But we don't. Heroes are celebrated because they are so rare.

And yet the mythic image of the good guy with the gun continues to dominate our public discourse, founded on a belief woven deep into our cultural fabric that we could all be Shane stepping out onto the dusty street to face off against a desperado, if only we had the chance and so long as we preserve our inalienable right to easy access to the right weapons.

There is something uniquely American about the image of the good guy with a gun—and make no mistake, we do have a collective image of him; his silhouette is etched as deeply in our national psyche as the picture we conjure when we think of serial killers. He—and in our minds, it's almost always a he—is steely eyed and determined, cool and fearless. We can't always see his face, and when we do it's often a reflection of our own, or at least the face we wish we could show to the world. But we know him by his deeds. He acts in the instant, not out of some mindless rage or panic but drawing his quiet strength and deadly grace from some inner well of virtue that would flow inside all of us if we only had his faith. He's David standing up to Goliath—an image Willeford summoned for me when he was describing his showdown with the killer in Sutherland Springs—or one of a dwindling "remnant . . . chosen by grace" and called upon to act on our behalf at a moment of absolute peril. By caprice of fortune, or, if you prefer, by divine right, he carries "a rod of iron"—an image plucked directly out of the very last book in that old Bible on my shrink's bookshelf, the book of Revelation, the same ancient text that so fascinated the killer at Simon's Rock College.

Never mind that the statistics don't necessarily support the myth. In many people's imagination, he's our last best hope, an American archangel with a flaming sword, an instant messiah with a full magazine riding in not on clouds of glory but on gun smoke and a muzzle flash.

If that sounds overly religious, that's because it is. The truth is, since the beginnings of America the sacred and the profane, God and guns, have been joined at the hip in American law and custom. For all the talk about the Second Amendment and its guarantee that we all have the right to be the "good guy with a gun" if we can find the courage, many of us—millions of us, in fact—believe with perfect faith that the Bill of Rights merely describes that right; it didn't create it, the Creator did. Indeed, if anything, that conflation of faith and firepower has only become more acute in recent decades. The culture war that has raged in America for almost two generations has always been, to some degree, a sectarian conflict. On abortion, on gay marriage, the debate more often has been about values believed to have been handed down from on high than about policy decisions made in Washington or in fifty state capitols. That's particularly true when it comes to the debate about the role of guns in American society. And there are those who believe that the increasingly sectarian nature of that debate has made it more difficult to reach a consensus on how best to respond to the escalating death toll from this so distinctly American epidemic of gun violence.

Chapter 8

I Cling to My Gun, You Cling to Yours

And he shall rule them with a rod of iron.

Revelation 2:27

I T'S A VAST expanse of hardwood forest and stands of brooding hemlocks, of gnarled rhododendrons clinging to the sides of the bluestone cliffs that loom above tumbling mountain streams. The deer are plentiful here. So are the bobcats and the bears. There are even those who claim, without much evidence, that the last of the catamounts, the Eastern mountain lion, extirpated from Pennsylvania more than a century ago, still stalks these woods. Rugged, seemingly remote, bisected by an interstate highway, of course, but otherwise it's a place apart, a place where you can imagine that you're far removed from the modern world. If some unseen hand suddenly dropped you here, you'd never know that you were less than an hour and a half from Midtown Manhattan.

This forgotten corner of northeastern Pennsylvania, a half hour or so east of Scranton, has always been the kind of place where people could imagine that they might lose themselves if they wanted to, and if they were so inclined, might find themselves again, fundamentally transfigured. More than two hundred years ago, the Shakers, a small Christian sect intoxicated by the belief that the final judgment was at hand, tried to carve a community out of this rocky forest where they could await the Apocalypse. They eventually grew tired of waiting, and weary of trying to coax food out of the stones, and they left, but not, as legend has it, before wryly dubbing their collection of failed farmsteads the "Promised Land." In the first half of the nineteenth century, the firebrand abolitionist and publisher Horace Greeley, who embraced the religiously fraught concept of Manifest Destiny with an almost biblical zeal, also tried to establish a utopian community called the Sylvania Colony here, near the conflux of the Lackawaxen and Delaware Rivers. His colonists also ultimately surrendered to the harsh reality of this hardscrabble land and gave up. In the fifty years that followed, the land was scrubbed of timber, but the forest had the last word and came back with a vengeance.

More recently, this corner of Pennsylvania—dotted with small private communities originally envisioned as weekend retreats for New Yorkers and Philadelphians— has drawn a new kind of pilgrim. "Doomsday preppers" they're called, many of them refugees from the cities and suburbs to the south and east, who hoard firearms and canned goods in anticipation of some future disaster brought on by the hand of God or the perfidy of man. As local television reporter Andy Mehalshick noted in a 2017 report, they're a secretive and suspicious bunch, and there's no way to know for sure how many preppers there are in these woods, but "based on the information we gathered in our research, their numbers . . . are on the rise."[1]

These woods have also given shelter to killers. This is the same forest that the so-called Indian killer Tom Quick, a one-man tip of the spear for Manifest Destiny, prowled two hundred years ago, executing Native American women and children, and it was in these same woods, in 2015, that a cop killer who liked to dress like a Serbian soldier murdered one state police officer and wounded another in an unprovoked attack, and then hid out in these three hundred square miles of dense woods for forty-eight days before he was finally captured.

But these are also my woods, or so I like to tell myself. For more than twenty years my wife and children and I have lived at the edge of this forest, and I flatter myself that I know every rutted fire road and almost every faint deer track between the ghost town of Bushkill and the once-upon-a-time silk-making village of Hawley. Indeed, there's rarely a day that goes by between mid-October and the end of January that you won't find me somewhere in these woods, my .50-caliber flintlock rifle slung over my shoulder, the .45-caliber flintlock pistol I made out of parts I inherited from my late father stuffed into my belt. The hours I spend in these woods stalking deer are as close as I get to prayer. You cling to your God. I cling to mine. You cling to your gun. I'll cling to mine. Mine is almost certainly different from yours, but it's still my "rod of iron"—a talisman, a totem, or, if I'm to be perfectly honest, a fetish item, a representation in blued gunmetal of the man I'd someday like to become. It's hardly an offensive weapon, and it'd be next to useless for self-defense. It takes patience and practice just to learn to load it: you must carefully measure out the gunpowder, pour it into the barrel, seat a round ball made of lead and cloaked in wadding into the muzzle, tamp it down with your ramrod, then prime the pan with more powder. And once you've done all that, you have just one shot. The man I'd someday like to be can do all of that with a kind of steely grace, with a self-assuredness that borders on the supernatural, the God-given. He can fox-foot silently through the woods, getting close enough to an unsuspecting deer that he can dispatch her mercifully and quickly with a single round and then humbly give thanks to his maker and to the doe for her sacrifice.

Of course, that's not the man I am. You can often find the man I am muttering curses through his dentures as his frigid fingers fumble, spilling powder down the length of his barrel while missing the muzzle completely, or frantically searching for a lost round ball in the frozen leaves while a doe or a buck bounds over the nearest ridge, its white tail at half-staff, nature's way of signaling contempt more than alarm. I am not the man my God or my gun wants me to be. Not yet. Perhaps I never will be. But almost every day between mid-October and the end of January, I stalk these woods, filled with the faith and irrational optimism of a young novice monk that maybe someday I'll be able to live up to the expectations of both, that the "rod of iron" in my hand will help me become the man I want to be. It's an article of faith for me. You cling to your God. I'll cling to mine. I cling to my gun. You cling to yours.

I find myself mouthing those words aloud as I drive across the two-lane bridge that leads out of the forest and into the village of Newfoundland, a former logging town a few miles west of the land the Shakers forsook, a bit farther southwest from the colony Greeley's disciples abandoned. There, smiling beatifically from a billboard at the edge of town, is the spiritual inspiration for the most recent sect to stake a claim on building a fortress against the Apocalypse in these woods, the late Rev. Sun Myung Moon. In the picture he's dressed in fluorescent hunting orange, and in his hands he holds a shotgun. Though he's been dead for nearly six years by the time I drive into town on this unusually balmy morning in late February 2018, the billboard still wishes him a happy birthday.

The late Reverend Moon, of course, never set foot in these woods. But his son, Rev. Hyung Jin "Sean" Moon, the head of a renegade church that splintered off from the Unification Church after the elder Moon's death, a man regarded even within his own family as kind of an Absalom to the Rev. Sun Myung Moon's David, most certainly has.

It was here, upon these rocks at the edge of Newfoundland, that in 2014 the younger Moon built his church—or rather repurposed one built by the Catholics—and established it as the world headquarters of a sect that holds as one of its central tenets that it's not just a man's God-given right to bear arms, it's his sacred duty, an obligation imposed by the Almighty.

That's what brought me to Newfoundland on this sunlit February morning—two weeks to the day after a killer with an AR-15 murdered seventeen students in Parkland, Florida—on the very morning that the survivors of that massacre were set to return to the school.

That was the day the young cleric had chosen to summon hundreds of his faithful followers from far and wide for a sacramental gathering here in this forgotten little crossroads town in the forests of northeastern Pennsylvania.

It was officially "a commitment ceremony," a chance for some 250 couples to rededicate themselves to each other, to the church, and to the messianic legacy of the sect's founder. Colloquially, though, it was called "the blessing of the guns," and in a statement of fealty to the church's founding principle—that every man is a sovereign, subject to no authority but God, and is thus morally obliged to bear arms—each of those 250 couples brought with them a rifle—a "rod of iron," the church's leader called them.

"Each of us is called to use the power of the 'rod of iron' not to arm or oppress as has been done in satanic kingdoms of this world, but to protect God's children," Rev. Moon wrote in a statement announcing the armed pilgrimage.

And come they did.

Two by two.

Though they appeared harmless enough in their crowns and their flowing white gowns and prayer shawls billowing from beneath heavy down coats, their unloaded semiautomatic rifles, for the most part, safely secured in gun cases, they caused enough of a stir that the local school district cancelled classes for the day. The school district didn't explain why. But Ram Montanaro, a crown-be-decked, self-declared spokesman for the church who'd traveled south from Maine for the gathering, insisted it was not because the armed congregants posed a threat, but because the press of media that had gathered at the church did.

"The media presented more of a threat to the kids than we did," he tells me. "[The local families] have been living side by side with us for years now and they're fine with what we're doing." Though when pressed, he admitted that this was the first time the church had asked its flock to flock to Newfoundland toting AR-15s.

Though the Reverend Moon had insisted that it was just a fluke of the calendar that this ceremony was being held on the same day that the traumatized students at Marjory Stoneman Douglas High School were returning to their classes, he still drew on that mass shooting to underscore his point. "If the football coach who rushed into the building to defend students from the shooter with his own body had been allowed to carry a firearm, many lives, including his own, could have been saved," Moon said.[2]

Like much in America's fractious gun debate, that is

more a declaration of faith than a statement of empirical fact. There is no question that coach Aaron Feis acted with remarkable heroism that day when he raced toward the sound of gunfire and threw open the door to a darkened hallway on the west side of the school building only to find that the killer was on the other side, already poised to fire the fatal round.[3] Maybe the coach, framed in silhouette, the afternoon sun behind him, might have quickly targeted the killer in the gloom and the confusion, and maybe he would have found it in himself to shoot first. As former ATF SWAT team member David Chipman put it to me, perhaps he might have been able to overcome even a nanosecond of hesitation and would have been able "to shoot someone who looks like a student" and bring an end to the atrocity without the loss of any more lives. But that remains an open question, an article of faith.

Indeed, that faith—or at least the principle embodied by the idea that good guys with guns are ordained by God—is a central pillar for this eccentric sect in the woods of Pennsylvania.

That's what Montanaro, a pastor of his own congregation in New England, fervently believes, and with an evangelist's patient zeal, he is willing to spend all the time he needs with me to make sure I understand the principle.

He's an affable man, well into middle age, with a friendly, rapid-fire way of speaking and a big paw that envelopes mine in a warm handshake the moment he sees me. He projects an image of serenity, smiling benignly as he glances over toward the white wooden fence that surrounds the church, where, on the other side, a handful of members of a rival Christian sect—this one an antigun group led by a preacher from nearby New York State—have cherry-picked other verses from the same Bible Montanaro reads and cut-and-pasted them onto placards protesting the blessing of the guns.

Montanaro sees no need to confront them or to evict them from the edge of the church's property. He assures me that his equanimity is not in any way influenced by the fact that a few yards beyond them, two state police officers and a Wayne County sheriff's deputy—agents of government power, in his mind—lounge against the sides of their SUVs, casually sipping coffee but ready to snap into action in the unlikely event that a confrontation erupts. Instead, he makes it clear that he believes that he can be tolerant and magnanimous because on this issue—on the issue of guns—the good Lord is firmly on his side.

With his off-the-rack Sunday suit and an actual, honest-to-God dollar-store crown perched at a jaunty angle on his head, he conjures an image of a jovial late-night local cable pitchman selling you used cars or mattresses or big-screen televisions. But that's not what Montanaro of the Unification Church is selling here today. No. He's pitching a vision of America that's very different from the one I grew up believing in. Montanaro's vision of America is one of a nation that's always just one thirty-round magazine away from toppling into an authoritarian abyss or devolving into a jungle full of would-be predators, private and public, always crouched, always waiting to pounce. "Whenever you concentrate power in the hands of a few, that corrupts," he tells me cheerfully as he smiles toward the cops. "The idea is to produce locally understood, locally supported protection of the home. Government, as much as possible . . . should be local."

It's in service to that notion that the congregants are all urged to carry AR-15s, he says, a weapon that he admits is singularly warlike in appearance and serviceably warlike in practice. "Why the AR as opposed to some other weapon?" he asked rhetorically. "You could basically ask why does the military use the AR? Basically an AR is an M16; it's chosen by the military as the most effective, efficient, easy-to-clean, easy-to-handle weapon. . . .

So why would they choose it? They choose it because in combat situations you need to have that."

Was he expecting to find himself someday in open combat with the government of the United States, or the Commonwealth of Pennsylvania, or the thirteen full-time officers in the Wayne County sheriff's department? I ask. "No," he tells me. "And we hope not to. But you don't want your house to burn down either, do you?"

It's tempting to dismiss the disciples of Reverend Moon and their blessed AR-15s as cranks and eccentrics, to write them off as just one more strange sect taking root for a time in the woods of northeastern Pennsylvania, worshipping a kind of golden calf (though in this case, it's a golden calf pressed out of black aluminum and steel that's capable of accepting a thirty-round magazine), before the cult vanishes with barely a trace.

It would be easy to pretend that this group, with their dollar-store crowns and gossamer gowns, is so far outside the American mainstream when it comes to guns that they need not be taken seriously, that they can be ignored.

But strip away the crowns and the gowns, dress them instead in $2,000 Italian suits, and put them at the podium at the yearly Conservative Political Action Conference (CPAC) rather than on the altar of a church in the woods, and what they believe is, in sum and substance, virtually identical to the positions taken by millions of Americans. What are confessions of faith to some are policy positions to others, identical to those espoused and promulgated by the National Rifle Association and embraced by the state and federal lawmakers who draw support from the NRA.

In August 2019, just hours after a mass killer from Odessa (who had failed a gun store background check) went on a ten-mile killing spree in West Texas, the second mass public shooting in Texas that month, state representative Matt Schaefer, who has enjoyed an "A" rating from the NRA, opened fire on gun-control advocates with a burst of rapid-fire tweets citing God as the ultimate guarantor of the unfettered right to bear arms.

"'Do something!' is the statement we keep hearing," Schaefer wrote in a Twitter thread. "As an elected official with a vote in Austin, let me tell you what I am NOT going to do. I am NOT going to use the evil acts of a handful of people to diminish the God-given rights of my fellow Texans. Period. None of these so-called gun-control solutions will work to stop a person with evil intent. I say NO to 'red flag' pre-crime laws. NO to universal background checks. NO to bans on AR-15s, or high capacity magazines. NO to mandatory gun buybacks."[4]

While Schaefer's tweets may have sparked outrage among some, particularly in the wake of two bloody back-to-back atrocities in his home state of Texas, they were not unique. Not in recent American history, and not in our distant past. As the late associate justice of the Supreme Court Antonin Scalia wrote in 2008 in the landmark decision in *District of Columbia v. Heller*—the case that firmly established that the right to bear arms is an individual right that does not depend on membership in any kind of "well-regulated militia"—law and custom in America and in Britain have long held that the right to bear arms is a "natural right" that supersedes any man-made statute.

Among the more arcane sources Scalia drew upon was an eighteenth-century treatise written in London on England's game laws, in which the author asked rhetorically, "What law prevents the veriest pauper, if he can raise a sum sufficient for the purchase of it, from mounting his Gun on his Chimney piece, with which he may not only defend his Personal Property from the Ruffian, but his personal rights from the invader of them?"[5]

That pauper's right to arm himself, Scalia's argument

goes, was seen, even in the American colonies, as a natural right, one that was self-evident and endowed from the Creator. To bolster that argument, he cited an 1833 paper by William Alexander Duer, a newspaperman, lawyer, and son of a continental congressman, in which Duer concluded that every American colonist had from on high an inviolable "right . . . to keep arms for his defence, suitable to his condition and degree; which was the public allowance, under due restrictions of the natural right of resistance and self-preservation."[6]

Of course, like all rights, handed down from on high or not, the right to bear arms is subject to restrictions, Scalia wrote. Of course,

> the Second Amendment right is not unlimited. It is not a right to keep and carry any weapon whatsoever in any manner whatsoever and for whatever purpose. For example, concealed weapons prohibitions have been upheld under the Amendment or state analogues. The Court's opinion should not be taken to cast doubt on longstanding prohibitions on the possession of firearms by felons and the mentally ill, or laws forbidding the carrying of firearms in sensitive places such as schools and government buildings, or laws imposing conditions and qualifications on the commercial sale of arms.[7]

Indeed, he affirmed that it was well within the purview of state and federal legislatures to enact laws like the National Firearms Act of 1934, the first real American gun-control law, adopted in the wake of high-profile gangland killings like the first St. Valentine's Day Massacre, that curtailed private ownership of entire classes of firearms such as fully automatic rifles and sawed-off shotguns.

That level of nuance, however, is not reflected in the rote and rituals at the tiny church in Newfoundland any more than it is in the nationwide gun debate. As Tara Isabella Burton writes in a piece for the online publication *Vox*, the day after the Reverend Moon's gun-toting convocation in the forest, the event could and perhaps must be seen as an example of how the debate over the proliferation of certain types of firearms in America is as much a religious debate as it is a political one. "The intensity with which its members have embraced guns, a deeply religious weapon, an instrument of divine protection, should tell us something about America more widely," she writes. "Sean Moon is tapping into an existing truth of gun culture: that they have become fetishized and imbued with a wider cultural ritualistic significance."

It would be a stretch, of course, to describe the Rev. Sean Moon's renegade offshoot of his late father's global ministry as a part and parcel of the Evangelical movement in the United States. Indeed, it's open to debate whether to even consider it representative of the Unification Church as it was founded by Sun Myung Moon. Months after the convocation in Newfoundland, the pastor's own mother sued him in state court for copyright infringement, alleging that the younger Moon had hijacked his father's trademark symbol—a radiating sun—and modified it slightly, surrounding it with golden AR-15s, to advance what the lawsuit describes as his "gun centered theology and political agenda."[8]

But while his pro-gun theology may ruffle feathers within his own family, he is, on this issue at least, marching in lockstep with other Christian soldiers in the Evangelical movement.

According to a 2017 survey conducted by the Pew Research Center and analyzed by the publication *Christianity Today*, Evangelicals are significantly more likely than the general public to own firearms—41 percent of them are gun owners, compared with about 30 percent of the population at large—and those who own handguns are a bit more likely than other gun owners to carry them when they head out for an evening on the town or a Sunday morning in the pews.[9] Sixty-five percent of white Evangelical handgun owners say they carry their weapons regularly, compared with 57 percent of other gun owners. And in many cases, they have the blessings of their pastors.

As Texas pastor and media personality Robert Jeffress of the First Baptist Church of Dallas told Fox News in a November 6, 2017, interview, "I'd say a quarter to a half of our members are concealed carry. They have guns, and I don't think there's anything wrong with that. They bring them into the church with them."[10]

White Evangelical Christians are also more reluctant than the general population to embrace new or stiffer gun laws, even in the aftermath of mass shootings, the Pew study found. Forty-four percent of them believe that the current state and federal gun laws, a patchwork at best, are strict enough, and another 23 percent told pollsters those gun laws ought to be loosened. Compare these responses with the 56 percent of Americans overall who believe that the time has come for stricter gun regulation.[11]

That deep suspicion among members of what we tend to call the religious right, one of America's most consistently reliable voting blocs, has deep historic and cultural roots. It's surely been exploited—and even weaponized— in recent decades by the gun-rights lobby. The NRA, for example, was fronted for years by the late Charlton Heston, Hollywood's right-leaning Moses. They've rallied the religious right to oppose extending background checks to include sales at gun shows and between private sellers; they've fanned the right's religious fervor to stymie bills in Congress that would restore the 1994 assault weapons ban; and they've lobbied to push through state laws, like the one in Texas that became law the day after the Odessa massacre, that would ease restrictions on where and when people could carry firearms. The gun lobby has used the religious right to put the fear of God in lawmakers, who scrupulously follow the NRA's creed and have come to depend on the NRA's earthly riches to fund their campaigns.

But the NRA did not just tap a rock with a staff to make that wellspring of religious sentiment flow. The conflation of gun rights and religious identity existed well before there was an NRA, before there was even a nation, and it is likely to remain a powerful political force for the foreseeable future. As columnist Rich Lowry writes in a 2019 article for the *National Review*, "There is a limit to how far gun control can go in America and . . . proponents of new restrictions should be fully aware that they are tampering with a constitutionally protected individual right. The Second Amendment doesn't have lesser status than the First."[12]

I saw how deeply rooted that religious sensibility is and how it frames any discussion of potential gun control legislation in my chat with Stephen Willeford, the hero who faced off against the killer after the Sutherland Springs massacre in Texas. He believes with absolute certainty that he prevailed that day because the killer was outgunned, not by Willeford's AR-15 but by God's personal and direct intervention. He believes he had the courage to face the killer because God gave it to him, and he believes he had the skill and the hardware to challenge and ultimately chase the killer down the road because God has ordained that he should have them. Willeford clings to his God and to his guns, and he does it proudly.

There is nothing of the braggadocio about him, at least nothing that I could hear in my conversation with him. He'll freely tell you that he was "terrified" when the killer interrupted the killing and emerged from the church to trade rounds on the street with him. There is no chest pounding when he recounts his role in bringing that horror to an end. He never uses the word "hero" to describe himself. Instead, he sees himself as an imperfect vessel. He is as outraged as anyone that the Sutherland Springs murderer—a violent man with a documented history of cruelty and mayhem who should have been barred under existing law from legally purchasing firearms—was able to pass a background check because the Air Force failed to disclose that the killer had been court-martialed and convicted of threatening his wife and her child with a loaded gun.[13]

But in Willeford's religious and political worldview, efforts to keep guns out of the hands of men like that could also risk staying God's hand, preventing the Almighty from using men like Willeford to stop them. He's skeptical of statistics and studies like the FBI's analysis of active shooters that show how rare it is for good guys with a gun to actually alter the outcome of public shootings. He argues, simply, "There are a lot more good guys with guns than bad guys." And he is deeply suspicious of any effort to tighten background checks or—God forbid—ban semi-automatic rifles or handguns, or of proposals that would require that those weapons be licensed or registered with authorities. That, he argues, would be the first step on the slippery slope to confiscation.

It's strange. As I was speaking with Willeford, it struck me that this decent, honorable, God-fearing, compassionate family man is a solid and respected member of his community who has sailed and would sail through any background check no matter how rigorous. Few if any of the proposals that have been floated to prevent killers from getting their hands on weapons of war would be likely to pry Stephen Willeford's fingers from around his rifles. Nor am I convinced that they should. There's not much in the grand scheme of things that Willeford and I would agree on, theologically or politically. Yet I walked away from that conversation convinced that there is not a weapon on earth I would not trust in Stephen Willeford's hands.

The problem is Stephen Willeford and Ram Montanaro and millions of God-fearing Americans like them don't trust me. Or more to the point, they don't trust people like me.

They have no faith that those who advocate stricter regulations on semiautomatic weapons, who favor more robust and more expansive background checks, or who call for a ban on extended-round magazines will not ultimately come and take their guns in what they believe is an affront to both Scripture and the Second Amendment that borders on blasphemy. So, like the zealous remnant described in the book of Isaiah, they hold fast, prepared to resist any initiative that they believe would signal the start of a campaign to undermine their sacred, natural right—which they perceive as a duty—to arm themselves as best they can against the perils of a perfidious world.

They cling to their God, and I cling to mine. They cling to their guns, and I cling to mine.

And in the meantime, the body count rises.

CHAPTER 9

The Fog
of War in
Peacetime

There's a wonderful phrase: "The fog of war." What
"the fog of war" means is: war is so complex it's beyond the ability of the human mind to comprehend
all the variables. Our judgment, our understanding, are not adequate.

Former US defense secretary Robert McNamara

Y ou'd think by now we'd have a word for it, a word
to describe the way the horror, the trauma, the confusion,
and the misconceptions spider-web out from the scene of
a mass public shooting in a digital instant, touching not
just those who are at ground zero but all of us, turning
millions of us into survivors or witnesses to an atrocity
in real time.

Trauma is one word, yes. So is terror. And chaos. In
combat they call it the fog of war. But we have no word
for the fog of war in peacetime.

You can see how profoundly the trauma of the fog
of war in peacetime affects even those who are trained
to face it. It's etched in the blank stare of the veteran
police officer we met in chapter 3, who, when faced with

the brutal massacre of children in his hometown, simply erased the memory. "I took the perimeter," he insists. You can hear it in the creak of the stairs late at night, as the first cop through the door at the massacre at West Nickel Mines pads to his sleeping daughter's bedroom.

You can feel the awful weight of it in the voice of a young police officer, summoned to Santa Fe High School near Galveston, Texas, in the moments after a shooting, ordered to hold the line, to be part of a force deployed in accordance with best police practices to stop the killing so that he and his comrades could stop the dying. All the while his own mother, a substitute teacher at that school, lay dead, or near dead, inside. "I'm supposed to protect and serve people," he later told his family attorney. "I couldn't even protect my own mother."

Indeed, in this fog of war in peacetime, we are demanding that our first responders, our police officers, our EMTs, our firefighters, face horrors on their home turf as great as any they'd find on the bloodiest foreign battlefield. That's something we haven't asked American soldiers to do at least since the Civil War, and yet we demand that our first responders do it.

We look away when they stumble out of the gun smoke and blood and double over, retching into the bushes, as police officers reportedly did when a combat veteran armed with a .45-caliber Glock 21, a cache of extended magazines he had smuggled across the state border from Nevada, and a knife killed twelve people before killing himself at the Borderline nightclub in Thousand Oaks, California, on November 7, 2018. Among the dead, as we'll see later in this chapter, was Tel Orfanos, an ex-sailor who'd already been traumatized just over a year earlier when he'd helped pull the wounded off the killing field below the towering Mandalay Bay Resort and Casino in Las Vegas during what remains the highest-casualty mass public shooting in our history.

The Borderline, that young man's mother and father, Mark and Susan Orfanos told me, was supposed to be his haven, his "safe space." It's a grim measure of our times that a young military veteran had heroically faced combat twice in his life, and both times it was at home. It's a measure of that young man himself that even though he had somehow escaped the initial onslaught and had gotten out of the nightclub, he raced back inside to save others and confront the murderer. When responders found Tel Orfanos's body, they discovered that not only had he been shot, he had also been stabbed once in the neck, an indication, the coroner told his grieving mother, that Tel had gone down fighting. It's deathly cold solace, but it gives his mother some shred of comfort to think that he didn't die afraid. "I tell myself that Tel was so angry that this person was doing what he was doing that he just flew at him," Susan Orfanos tells me through her tears, lapsing for just an instant into the present tense, a sign that the trauma is not, and perhaps never will be, in the past. "I don't want my son to be afraid," she says. "Or to hurt. And I try to tell myself that Tel would have been so angry, he would have confronted that man, and it would have been over in seconds."

In the aftermath of these atrocities we focus, understandably perhaps, on the killers and their possible motives, or, more compassionately, we recite the names of the wounded and the dead. And so we should. But often our incantations drown out other voices we should listen to: we should hear them out of compassion, yes, but out of self-interest as well. There's much that we must give back to those first responders, like the ones who staggered, drenched in blood and choking on gun smoke, out of the Pulse nightclub in Orlando, Florida, after a steroid-abusing gunman with a history of alleged domestic violence, a valid state firearms license, and an image of himself as an Islamic avenger opened fire and killed forty-nine people at the gay-friendly nightclub, a place the killer was reportedly known to frequent.

Deborah Beidel, a professor who runs a clinic at the University of Central Florida that treats first responders, spoke to ProPublica in an article detailing symptoms of PTSD among those who dashed into the Pulse nightclub on our behalf. As she puts it, "There are just some events that are so horrific that no human being should be able to just process that and put it away."[1]

The hidden, psychic wounds of post-traumatic stress on our police officers and first responders put a terrible burden on them, and responding to this is a challenge to us all.

And when, as we saw at Parkland, one of our officers, one of our defenders, fails for whatever reason to rise to the moment, we vilify him and sometimes even prosecute him. That too is a burden we spare our combat soldiers for the most part, says Lt. Daniel Jewiss, who as lead investigator of the Sandy Hook massacre has seen up close and personal the impact the stress of these atrocities can place on officers, immediately and in the long term.

There isn't a commander in the United States military who would ever dream of sending an untested soldier alone into one-on-one combat with a heavily armed enemy, and yet we insist that our police be always prepared to do just that. A novice soldier in a foreign war may well flinch or fail, but the next day or the day after, that soldier will likely be sent out on a patrol again. Soldiers who have a lapse get a chance to redeem themselves in their own eyes and the eyes of their comrades. "We . . . have really good soldiers that freeze or slow it down," Jewiss says. "And you know what? They get some remedial training. . . . They . . . get another chance two days later when they're back on patrol."

There are no second chances for police on American soil, he says.

"With us, it might be a once-in-a-career choice and then you live with that."

Forever.

Take a few steps back from ground zero in any of these attacks, and the fog of war in peacetime is every bit as poisonous and impenetrable. You needn't go far. Just travel a few yards down the hallway from the classrooms at Sandy Hook where children were murdered to another classroom where frightened children huddled, fearing that they would be next. What can you say, Jewiss asks, to a father whose nine-year-old son is tortured by nightmares, who is facing years, perhaps decades, of therapy to come to grips with the traumatic memory of hearing gunshots and the awful silence between them, a child who is stalked in his sleep by the image of a man all dressed in black, his face obscured, pulling at his classroom door?

You can tell him that it wasn't the murderer trying to get to him, but rather a cop making sure the door was locked, making sure that the child and his classmates were indeed safe before moving on to make sure other children were, too. And that would be absolutely true, Jewiss tells me. It was indeed a cop who was there only to protect him. But would that knowledge exorcise the picture of a maniacal, faceless killer all dressed in black that possesses this child's dreams?

When your nightmares are forged out of gunmetal, they don't easily bend to fit the facts.

And those facts are often hard to see in the fog of trauma. Eyewitness accounts are notoriously unreliable, Jewiss tells me, and that's especially true after an atrocity like a mass public shooting.

Even those who are right there, who witness firsthand the horrors, are often so overwhelmed by them—so lost in the deathly silence between gunshots—that they sometimes pluck unrelated images out of the ether, things they've heard, or they summon images out of their own nightmares to fill in the spaces in their memories, to find explanations to make sense of the senseless and inexplicable, Jewiss tells me. And instantly, those are part of the story.

Thus a mask appears over a killer's bare face at a school in Connecticut when there is none. Or a misheard declaration of faith from beneath a table in a school library in Colorado becomes a legend. Or a long black trench coat seen from a distance and then quickly discarded becomes an emblem, a symbol, an icon so powerful that years, decades later, another killer, say at a high school in Texas, will choose to wear one. Perhaps he knows that in the narrative we've built that costume will make him seem more terrifying in our eyes, and our fear gives him power.

It would be challenging enough if those misconceptions were confined to the crime scene. But they are not. Not now, not in our 24/7 media world. Almost instantaneously after a mass atrocity, the national media appears on scene, at a roadside in Odessa or an Amish schoolyard in Pennsylvania, places that they wouldn't have been able to find with a divining rod in the days before GPS.

To be sure, there is a debate to be had over the question of whether the media's laser-like focus on mass public shootings distorts what is, admittedly, a comparatively rare type of atrocity and makes it appear more common than it is; or worse, that their coverage might inspire future killers.

As researcher Jacklyn V. Schildkraut writes in "Mass Murder and the Mass Media":

Nearly as soon as the first shot is fired, the news media already are rushing to break coverage of rampage shooting events, the likes of which typically last days or, in the more extreme cases, weeks. Though rampage shootings are rare in occurrence, the disproportionate amount of coverage they receive in the media leads the public to believe that they occur at a much more regular frequency than they do. Further, within this group of specialized events, there is a greater tendency to focus on those that are the most newsworthy, which is categorized most often by those with the highest body counts. This biased presentation can lead to a number of outcomes, including fear of crime, behavioral changes, and even copycat attacks from other, like-minded perpetrators.[2]

Other observers argue that the latest deadly events in an ongoing series of atrocities deserve the kind of attention the media grants them. According to the *Washington Post* editorial board, mass murder claimed the lives of 1,196 people between August 1966 and August 11, 2019, and the epidemic would kill another 53 people before the month of August was out.[3]

The media coverage, of course, is imperfect. Sometimes it's deeply flawed. It's happened time and time again, at Sandy Hook and Parkland, at Columbine and Poway. A man or woman on the street repeats a story they heard to a reporter, and then a second source who heard the same story repeats it again, and then a third. Often they're accurate, at least on balance. Sometimes they're not. It's hard to suss out the difference between fact and rumor in the fog of war in peacetime. It's harder when the competitive crush of a media scrum adds even more chaos to an already chaotic and confusing crime scene. And it's harder still when all of that is happening in unfamiliar territory. Ask any reporter who's ever worked a beat: it takes years to develop the kind of trust between a reporter and a police chief, or spokesperson, that allows the official to pull the reporter aside and warn them that the story they've been told has not been confirmed and may indeed be wrong. That kind of trust isn't built in a day.

So, absent that kindly guidance, you trust the sources you do have. You tell yourself that the story you're telling has passed journalistic muster. It's come from multiple sources. The stories make sense and most of the time they're told sincerely. There is no maliciousness in it, not on the part of the source, not on the part of the reporter, not usually. And you test them against your own knowledge and understanding. And therein lies the rub. You see, we reporters have been raised with the same myths everybody else has, for decades. Yes, we are predisposed to follow bloodshed and body counts.

"If it bleeds, it leads." It's an old saying in my business. But "it" doesn't bleed. People bleed. And I can tell you from personal experience, it doesn't matter how much of a cartoon, 1930s honey-get-me-rewrite hardass a reporter like me might think he or she is, if you parachute into somebody else's neighborhood to cover somebody else's nightmare—whether it's the slaying of a bodega owner in the middle of the night in Paterson, New Jersey, or a mass shooting at a school—it affects you. Cover the murder of even one child, and I promise you, after deadline you're going to tiptoe up to your sleeping daughter's bedroom and hold her in the dark, not because she's crying but because you are.

So you report the story. Often it's accurate. Sometimes the facts will later show you that it's not, and you'll dutifully and professionally write an updated story or issue a clarification or a correction. But by that time, as often as not, the old story has already been firmly woven into the epic myth we've been murmuring in the fog for five decades. A misheard declaration of faith instantly becomes an article of faith. A hero is acclaimed, anointed, rightly so, though the credit for his courageous act is given to his gun rather than his character, when, if all the evidence were known, the facts may be far murkier. A trench coat becomes an inky cloak for a mythical villain, a costume another killer might assume. A manifesto, cut and pasted from the one that came before it, becomes a motive. A reason. But there is no reason.

And the fog spreads. There aren't enough police barricades or enough rolls of bright yellow police tape in the world to confine it to the perimeter of a crime scene, not in a world as deeply interconnected as ours. Not in a world where news—imperfect and incomplete—can circle the globe in the time it takes a dying heart to stop beating. And it isn't just the mass media that spreads the fog. Consider this: when the cops finally made it into the charnel house that had been the Pulse nightclub, it wasn't just the blood and the stench of murder that knocked them back on their heels. It was the surreal sound of so many cellphones, left behind by those who had fled the massacre or still in the hands or pockets of those who didn't, chirping, buzzing, ringing, some playing a macabre merengue. And who was calling? Everyone they knew.[4]

When they found Tel Orfanos's body on the floor of the Borderline nightclub, he still had his phone. There were "over a thousand texts on it," his father tells me. "There was a couple hundred . . . voicemails—people calling him from all over the country who knew him . . . asking him if he was OK."

That's hundreds of people—perhaps more than a thousand—from every corner of the nation, touched in real time by the trauma of one death in one mass shooting.

Multiply that by all the dead and all the wounded and all those who have been spared in all the churches and nightclubs and synagogues and schools, all the malls and Walmarts and movie theaters, and you see how the trauma of these "rare" atrocities spreads like a virus across the globe. Indeed, the atrocity at the Borderline, just down the road from the Orfanoses' home, had already touched people across the country before Mark and Susan Orfanos had even learned that it had happened. They'd sent their son their usual goodnight text and had gone to bed, only to be awakened to their nightmare at two a.m. by a phone call from a close family friend on the other side of the country, Tel's godmother, who had just learned of the massacre from the news. They immediately flipped on the television and desperately called their son.

"His voicemail box was full," Susan tells me.

In our hyperconnected digital world, linked by social media and the phones in our hands, the immediacy of the trauma is felt by thousands, tens of thousands, perhaps millions, in an instant. Even before the first breathless reporter arrives on the scene—even before the cops do, sometimes—Twitter explodes; grainy cellphone videos, punctuated by the sound of gunfire or of a terrified survivor weeping or screaming, ricochet around the world. It's horror with a hashtag. There is no context, no big picture. You can never make sense of the senseless, and when you're running for your life, you don't even try. There are just jagged shards of terror. Indeed, as we saw at Christchurch and at Pulse, sometimes the killers even broadcast themselves on social media to amplify the horror and to bask in it. And the fog of war in peacetime, and the trauma that lurks in the mist, spreads.

"One does not have to be a combat soldier in war, or visit a refugee camp in Syria or the Congo to experience trauma," psychiatrist and researcher Bessel van der Kolk writes in the prologue to his landmark book *The Body Keeps the Score: Brain, Mind, and Body in the Healing of Trauma*. He is writing specifically about those in the closest concentric rings to trauma survivors: their families, their friends, and their acquaintances. But he notes that the effects radiate out from there, touching those who know them, until, at last, it can infect "our histories and our cultures."[5]

It's a drifting fog, and it's boundless. I caught a glimpse of the spreading fog myself not so very long ago, when, in the wake of another deadly active-shooter situation, an old friend, a woman I had not spoken with in years, reached out to me on Facebook from across the country just hours after she had watched her best friend die from a killer's bullet. I called her immediately, and we talked for about an hour. I'm not going to tell you what was said. I'm not even going to tell you which of the many active-shooter situations she had survived. None of that is any of your business. She didn't reach out to me because I'm a reporter, or because she knew I was working on this book, and I didn't call her for information, or for another story for a book already far too full of them. She reached out to an old friend because she had experienced an unimaginable trauma and was in pain, and I called her back to share that pain and to offer what solace I could. And the fog of war in peacetime and the trauma spread further.

And that fog does not just spread through space, it also spreads across time. It travels from one generation to the next. You see that in your own children's eyes, hear it in their voices when they tell you about the lockdown drills they had at school.

Thousands of American schools—95 percent of the schools in the nation, according to a report published by *Education Week* in 2018—now conduct some version of the drills.[6] Students are instructed either to hide silently, out of sight of the locked classroom door, or to follow the protocols known as ALICE: an acronym for Alert, Lockdown, Inform, Counter, Evacuate, which boils down to three words, "run, hide, fight." In some cases police officers or school officials prowl the hallways, playing the role of a school shooter in a grotesque dress rehearsal for an atrocity. Police and experts consider these lockdowns best practices, and, as we saw in the case in Richmond, Indiana, at the beginning of chapter 6, when they're triggered by a real threat, they can save lives.

In other cases, of course, they don't. Just weeks before the mass murder at Parkland, the students there underwent a lockdown drill. It didn't matter. Eleven of the seventeen killed were gunned down on the first floor before they ever had a chance to take cover inside their classrooms, according to a minute-by-minute reconstruction of the slayings compiled by the police and presented to the state commission investigating the event.[7]

Some experts worry that the whole notion of clustering children in a classroom might simply make them easier targets in the event that a killer does breach a classroom door. As one investigator, a veteran of a mass school shooting, told me in the sparse, utilitarian language of a cop, "Now via lockdown procedures we've got a bunch of kids in one corner of the room. [That] works against them."

For now, however, the best practice is the best hope we've got. And it's put into practice frequently.

Although school shootings may be rare, actual lockdowns, sometimes triggered by a perceived threat in the neighborhood rather than an actual event, are not. According to a *Washington Post* report, 4.1 million children and youths in America experienced a lockdown in the 2017–2018 school year.[8] Most were false alarms. But the impact of them, combined with the psychological effects of the regularly scheduled rehearsals for death, may be taking a profound toll on our children, psychologists tell us.

Imagine a childhood spent in a classroom where there's a poster featuring the words to "Twinkle, Twinkle, Little Star" rewritten to reflect our modern terror: "Lockdown, lockdown, lock the door, shut the lights off, say no more." You needn't imagine it. As Erika Christakis wrote in the *Atlantic* in March 2019, there is just such a poster in at least one kindergarten in Massachusetts.[9]

Indeed, we have institutionalized trauma. In Michigan, for example, by the 2021–2022 school year, the 860 high school students who attend Fruitport High School will be able to carry their bullet-resistant backpacks to a brand-new $48 million school building designed with curved walls, impact-resistant glass, and doors that lock with the touch of a smartphone, all designed to thwart a potential school shooter.[10] That's one metric of the impact of a national trauma that goes far beyond the number of actual mass public shootings.

Here's another: according to a Pew poll taken in the weeks after the February 14, 2018, murders at Marjory Stoneman Douglas High School in Florida, a majority of American kids between the ages of thirteen and seventeen—57 percent of them—live with the fear that they might someday be gunned down by a stranger or a classmate at school.[11] Or at the movies. Or at the mall. For one in four of those kids, it's a serious worry. Their parents are worried too. Sixty-three percent of the parents of those children, the Pew poll tells us, harbor at least some small fear that one day they'll get a text from their child, sent from the darkness of a supply closet or from beneath a library table in the middle of the day, and that will be the last they'll ever hear from them.

It's always been true that trauma is handed down from one generation to the next, as a kind of perverse heirloom, a secondhand horror transmitted through time. As van der Kolk writes, "Since time immemorial we have rebounded from our relentless wars, countless disasters (both natural and man-made), and the violence and betrayal in our own lives. But traumatic experiences do leave traces, whether on a large scale (on our histories and cultures) or close to home, on our families, with dark secrets being imperceptibly passed down through generations."[12]

But now it's transmitted openly, directly. It's written in our school policies and voted on by school boards: "This is the coat a school shooter wears"; "This is where you hide when he shows up"; "This is where you run when he finds you." It's monumentalized in the blueprints for a new school building designed to slow down a killer with a rapid-fire, high-powered rifle but not necessarily to stop him, a $48 million project to buy a few precious seconds in the fog of war in peacetime. We can offer our thoughts and prayers that it will never be tested. Odds are it won't. But it might. And even if it isn't, fifty years from now that building will still be standing, a testament to how far the trauma of these mass public shootings has spread, across the nation, across generations.

Few people in America have been better prepared, by cruel fate and rigorous training, to weigh the long-term impacts of the fog of war in peacetime than Roger Friedman. It's not just that the clinical psychologist, social worker, and teacher at the University of Maryland School of Social Work has studied the lasting effects of all manner of trauma on those who have been wounded by them, both as civilians and first responders. It's not just that he's the author of several important treatises on the epidemic of trauma. He's also been touched by it. His closest friend as a child, Paul Sonntag, was murdered from the Tower in Austin when a failed student and ex-Marine jacked a round into his Remington and fired the first shots in what has become an ongoing atrocity. Sonntag, an eighteen-year-old graduate of Stephen F. Austin High School, wasn't even a student at the University of Texas. Neither was his girlfriend, eighteen-year-old Claudia Rutt. He was still on summer vacation, preparing for his freshman year at the University of Colorado. She would have started classes a short time later at Texas Christian University. They were just on the Drag, the commercial strip adjacent to the campus, heading toward the university co-op to browse the record collection when they were murdered.

Friedman was not with them that day. But he tells me that they've been with him often, in his mind, in the fog, since then. One of the most insidious things about the fog of war in peacetime is that all too often it spreads in silence, the silence between gunshots, enveloping you without you even realizing it. Though he doesn't use those precise words, Friedman writes eloquently about it in the book he coauthored on that first modern mass public shooting. In a far-ranging discussion with me, he spoke of how, as deeply as he had been touched—traumatized—by the murders, how deep his own sense of loss was, he had repressed it, buried it. "I was teaching and lecturing and speaking with students—graduate students—for twenty-five years," he says. And yet

> it wasn't until I started writing that book . . . that it even occurred to me to talk about my experience with trauma to those classes. I just repressed it.
> I didn't talk about it. I somehow disassociated from it, I didn't even . . . remember it. . . . That's the kind of disassociation and isolation that we go through. Everyone. Of all the survivors, someone like me should be much more keenly aware of this stuff. But you're not in your own life. Until something wakes you up.

That is, of course, a perfectly human response. It was for him, just as it was to a far greater degree for the SWAT team member at Sandy Hook who utterly erased from his memory the image of the unimaginable carnage he had witnessed in that classroom. It's a response wired into us, Friedman says. We all have a primordial instinct to fight or flee, and if that fails, to simply deny what has happened, what is happening. It's the thing that saved us from the predations of a wild natural world, he says. To survive, our bodies evolved with a limbic system, a kind of "internal warning system in the brain that was meant to be set off episodically and briefly to save us from the tiger coming down the road," Friedman says.

But what happens when the tiger is one of us, when he goes to your school or works beside you at your job, when he frequents the same mall where you buy your child's new bullet-resistant backpack for school, or when, for reasons very different from yours, he likes the same movies you like? What if the warning that the tiger could strike at any moment is emblazoned in singsong words set to the tune of an ancient childhood ditty in your child's kindergarten classroom? What if the alert is broadcast by the mass media and repeated and distorted in the darker corners of the Internet? Then, he says, that ancient evolutionary early warning system is always on, always sounding the alarm.

Sometimes the memory of a recent mass public shooting starts to fade, as such memories often do, and that early warning system is reduced to a dull sound in the back of your mind. Other times, the alarm is shrill and terrifying. But for far too many of us, it's always there, making us ever-vigilant, sometimes dangerously hyper-vigilant, Friedman says, leaving us predisposed to over-react to some perceived threat. It's there for those of us who've endured the different but still uniquely American crime and gang-driven violence in our cities, and it's there for those of us who mistakenly believed that we were safer in our suburbs and rural areas.

What's more, Friedman says, this constant state of alert bordering on alarm threatens to drive each of us deeper into isolation. We suffer it alone, he tells me, and often we suffer in silence. "Trauma creates isolation between people because we don't want to talk about it. We don't want to be reminded of it. We don't want to reexperience it," he says.

What is true of those who are closest to the epicenter of an atrocity is true of us all, he tells me. If decades spent studying the effects of trauma on individuals as a psychologist and examining those effects more broadly as a sociologist have taught Friedman anything, it's that it is safe to assume that what a single person suffers is also suffered by all of us as a society.

"There absolutely is a national limbic system," he says. "It's the power of the social system and the media and the leadership in that system and the constant revving up about protection." And as we grapple with a seemingly endless series of atrocities, as isolated and yet deeply interconnected as we are, the trauma, the fog of war in peace slowly wraps around us all.

And in that fog, he says, we conjure myths and manufacture narratives. That, too, is something Friedman is uniquely qualified to understand. After all, it was his brother, songwriter Kinky Friedman, who, in the silence between gunshots after the Tower massacre, helped solidify the myth of what happened that day with his "ballad" to the murderer. It's worth noting that it wasn't until decades after that atrocity, decades after Kinky Friedman's song had been recorded, that the University of Texas symbolically ended that silence and erected a memorial to the dead and wounded and to the survivors. By that point, however, the myths had long been cast in stone. A survey by Rosa Eberly, the linguistics scholar we met in chapter 2, conducted long after the killings, found that for those students who knew anything at all about what had happened on the first day of August 1966, the first day of the modern era of mass public shooters, what little they knew had been derived mostly from Kinky Friedman's ahistorical ballad rather than from any vetted, authoritative source.

That's not surprising, Roger Friedman tells me. Trauma breeds silence and isolation, and in response to that trauma we create narratives. We fill in the blanks and try to give form to the silhouettes we spy in the fog.

We try to apply order to the chaos and imagine that we can find reasons for senseless slaughter: a video game, a manifesto, a trench coat, a tumor. We try to convince ourselves that we can see the killer coming, that we can recognize him by his age or his race, and we tell ourselves that amongst us are heroes who, armed as well as the killers themselves, will rise to protect us. We sometimes even convince ourselves that we have it in us to be that hero. We erect monuments to our fear and dedicate them as a school, turning a high school into a fortress in the hope that the design could slow a gunman, though few of us are still naïve enough to imagine it will stop him.

The myths we create, and the true stories we repeat, give us some shred of comfort, Friedman tells me. It's a frigid comfort to be sure, just as it is for Susan Orfanos, who takes what solace she can from her certainty that at least her son died angry and not frightened.

But what happens to all those comforting stories, all those myths that we cling to in the belief that they can make us safe, when a new kind of killer strips them all away? What happens to the half-century-old narrative we've created and embroidered with our collective trauma when the killer doesn't fit our profile or imagined picture of him? When he shows none of the warning signs we've come to expect? When he writes no manifesto and simply rides the elevator to the thirty-second floor of a tower far taller than the one in Texas and mercilessly begins a shooting, mowing down people by the hundreds with such rapid-fire weapons that there is no silence between gunshots?

His name was Stephen Paddock. There. I've said it. And this is the last time his name will be mentioned in this book.

CHAPTER 10

From
a Taller
Tower

MAYBE IT NEVER happened. Maybe, in the fog of war in peacetime, he had imagined it. Or worse, maybe he was trying to thrust himself into the national media spotlight, to snatch a shard of instant fame in the shattering aftermath of a savage mass murder. That thirst for fame runs deep in our culture, and it can make people do terrible things. It can tempt some to weave stories out of whole cloth, as any cop can attest, particularly in the wake of a historic atrocity. It can, as scholars like J. Reid Meloy who have studied mass shootings tell us, even spur others to commit mass murder.

Or maybe it really did happen. He was very specific about the time and place—the corner of Las Vegas Boulevard and Hacienda, at a bus stop within sight of the Mandalay Bay Resort and Casino, near the fif-teen-acre fenced-in venue where some 22,000 people had gathered for the final night of a three-day country music festival. It was 10:03 p.m. on October 1, 2017, he told police. He had been waiting for about three minutes for his bus when a red-haired man in a state of agita-tion approached him.[1] "Do you believe in God?" the red-haired man hissed through the space where his missing three front teeth had been. It seemed to him, he told police, that the agitated man glanced toward the tower-ing hotel, and then added, "Say a prayer for what's about to happen tonight."

The street-corner male Cassandra in black shorts and a sweater moved on, but not before asking the man wait-ing for the bus if he knew where to find tickets for the concert. He moved on also, when his bus arrived.

Two minutes later, what is, at least for now, the dead-liest mass shooting carried out by a single gunman in the history of the nation began. A compulsively secre-tive, gray-haired, sixty-four-year-old man—the son of a psychopath who was, authorities suspect, a psychopath himself—had obsessively planned every detail of the attack. Investigators would later report that he seemed to have taken great pains to mask his methods and his motives before opening fire on a crowded concert from a suite of ritzy rooms on the 32nd floor of the Mandalay Bay hotel. He had amassed the largest arsenal ever used in a mass public shooting—he had twenty-two semiautomatic rifles, fourteen of them fitted with bump-stock devices that made his legally purchased semiautomatics mimic machine guns and allowed him to fire 1,057 rounds into the panicked crowd below so quickly that when he pulled the trigger there was no silence between gunshots. He also carried a bolt-action rifle and the .38-caliber hand-gun he used to take his own life as police closed in on him, an act that he had also meticulously planned and carefully concealed in advance, authorities have concluded. By the time the shooting stopped, 58 people were dead or dying, not counting the murderer. At least 413 others were wounded by bullets or shrapnel, and approximately 360 more were injured in the mad rush to flee the carnage, according to the Las Vegas Metropolitan Police Department. There were 927 casualties in all.

It had taken about eleven minutes.

So secretive was the killer that no obvious red flags were waved, no overt signals accidentally sent or received. No dire alarm was raised—unless you count the cryptic warning of a street-corner Cassandra, who, if he existed at all, might in his agitation have issued the same warning to different strangers at a bus stop the day before, or the day before that. It's just that by a twist of fate or the alchemy of the odds, on that cloudless night he accidentally turned out to be right.

If you peer deeply enough into the police interviews with witnesses, including with those who'd known the killer, you can in hindsight see the faint traces of many of the traits we've learned to look for: the pathological narcissism, a sense of recklessness and remorselessness. He was obsessive. Competitive. He could be cold and manipulative and viewed others—including those closest to him—as objects to be used and then discarded. As Las Vegas police wrote in their 187-page report on the slayings, quoting his brother, the killer "needed to feel important and only cared how relationships would benefit him."[2] Look deeper and you can see the outline of the behaviors we've come to regard as warning signs, those moments when obsession becomes ideation and, as Meloy tells us, when that ideation crosses the line into preparation. You can faintly see the stresses in his life; there usually are among mass public shooters. Of course, stresses are usually apparent in all of our lives. And you can spot the clues that signal that he was scouring the Internet for a target for his attack, searching for large, exposed, outside venues where thousands would be likely to gather, and that he was arming himself for it. In the months leading up to the massacre, he went on a gun-buying spree, stocking up on an arsenal of deadly weapons and all the ammunition he would need.

But, as analysts deeply steeped in the details of the Las Vegas massacre conclude, you can also see evidence that he carefully masked all of those behaviors. As the FBI analysts put it in a brief statement issued at the end of a yearlong probe into the killer's mindset, "Throughout his life he went to great lengths to keep his thoughts private and that extended to his final thinking about this mass murder."[3]

It was as if he knew the drill as well as we do and consciously sought to conceal and control all of those warning signs, as if he was trying to confound all our methods and challenge all our myths, as if he knew that if he did so, that would compound the horror of a horrible atrocity. It was as if he'd figured out that if he could strip away all the frigid comforts we've come to cling to, if he could reduce mass murder to its brutal basics, if he could unleash more bullets from more and more-deadly weapons, if he could kill and wound more people from a perch on a taller tower, then he could leave us nothing to cling to but the horror of the mass murder itself. Then he could kill every killer that came before him.

If the murderer who climbed the Tower in Texas on August 1, 1966, was really Patient Zero in the epidemic of mass public shootings that has wounded us for half a century, if he was indeed the first modern mass public shooter, then perhaps we can describe the killer who climbed a taller tower in Las Vegas on October 1, 2017, as the first postmodern mass shooter, a mass murderer who didn't even bother to explain.

He didn't try to wrap himself in any ideological cloak.

His two ex-wives and his current girlfriend couldn't remember him ever discussing politics, or even gun laws, not with them and not with anyone else. He never expressed any animus toward minorities, as other killers have. Sometime before the shooting he mentioned in passing to his girlfriend, an immigrant from the Philippines, that he was pleased with the new administration in Washington because he believed it would "do something to stop illegal immigration,"[4] but there is no indication that it was an issue of any great importance to him, and he certainly made no effort to use it to justify his murderous instincts—as the killers in Christchurch, and in Pittsburgh, and the murderer in El Paso in 2019 would.

He left no manifesto. Not even a suicide note, though authorities are now convinced that he planned all along to kill himself at a moment of his choosing, after the massacre, as if he wanted to taunt with his silence the officers who would blast open the door to his hotel room and find his body. In fact, the only writings of any kind they found when they searched the killer's rooms were a couple of hastily scrawled notes: soulless, technical marksman's notations in longhand, gauging distance and elevation, murder on an unimaginable, massive scale reduced to a handful of arcane numbers.[5]

He had no prior criminal record. Indeed, the Las Vegas Metropolitan Police Department concluded in its detailed report on the investigation that the killer "did not commit a crime until he fired the first round into the crowd" at the Route 91 Harvest music festival.[6]

Nor was there any official record of a psychiatric or psychological history that would have barred him from purchasing a gun—or forty-seven of them, the total of his arsenal found in the hotel room and the two homes he owned—or that would have marked him, even to those who thought they were closest to him, as a potential mass murderer. An autopsy studied what was left of his brain after he sent a .38-caliber bullet through it. There was no tumor.

Though his personal physician later told police that he suspected that the killer might have bipolar disorder, a condition that affects millions of Americans who never harm anyone, he was never formally diagnosed with it, and he resisted the doctor's efforts to get him to take anti-depressants, but agreed reluctantly to accept a prescription for anti-anxiety medication. He was not known to abuse drugs or alcohol.

He was, however, a high-stakes gambler, a fixture at several Vegas casinos, where he would often spend hours on end in front of a flotilla of video poker games, sometimes winning, sometimes losing—and losing big. Between 2015 and 2017, investigators say, he paid out $600,000 to casinos. He could afford to. He was, after all, a comparatively wealthy man. Two years before the mass murder, he had $2.1 million stashed across fourteen separate bank accounts.[7] Though his wealth had been significantly depleted through his gambling losses, by his gifts to his girlfriend—he had sent her on a trip home to the Philippines and wired her a substantial amount of money just before the attack—and by some $95,000 he had spent on guns and paraphernalia, he still had more than half a million in the banks when he rode up the service elevator to the 32nd floor of the Mandalay Bay hotel, as VIPs often do. Nor was he, by all accounts, a sweaty-palmed compulsive gambler. He was obsessive, yes, according to the casino employees who knew him, but focused and methodical and analytical. "He seemed to be working at a higher level mentally than most of the people I run into gambling," one former casino executive told the *New York Times* in an October 7, 2017, profile of the killer.[8] But he also rigidly demanded that everyone acknowledge his status. "He acted like everybody worked for him and like he was above the others," the executive told the paper.

In fact, his family members told authorities that he had always been that way: calculating, cold, a narcissist. His youngest brother once said of him that he was "the king of micro-aggression," who could, when necessary, appear considerate, but only when it suited his purposes.[9] He and his brothers were raised in Southern California by a single mother, after his father, a bank robber who had once made the FBI's Ten Most Wanted Fugitives list—the agency described him at the time as a psychopath—was sent to prison. There is no obvious indication that the sins of the father were visited on the son. The killer was seven years old when his father was imprisoned and rarely saw him after that.

He had no record of grossly aberrant behavior as a child or a teen. On balance, he seemed just like everybody else, if sometimes a little more so. He was a good student, though even then he was seen as arrogant and cold, secretive and occasionally cruel, but never violent.

As he grew older he became single-mindedly preoccupied with escaping the lower middle class to which he was born and set his sights on becoming rich. As a young man he leapfrogged through various jobs that he imagined would lead him to riches, with stops along the way in nondescript desk jobs at the IRS and in the aerospace industry, but he grew bored and frustrated before finally, in the 1980s, turning to real estate, where he achieved his goal and, a few years later, retired a wealthy man.

Easily bored, he plunged into one hobby after another, usually solitary pursuits like scuba diving or flying, and then, authorities said, he'd lose interest just as quickly, sell off his equipment, and move on.

So in October 2016 when he began obsessively stockpiling weapons and ammunition, no one who knew him thought anything of it. They never imaged that he was preparing for a massacre. Why would they? Even his girl-friend, who on occasion helped him unload the firearms and ammunition he'd purchased from the trunk of his car, just figured guns were his latest toys, and sooner or later they too would end up discarded.

On average, the FBI tells us, active shooters experience between three and four stress events in advance of their crimes, and the killer at Las Vegas was no exception.[10] Nor are any of us. Yes, he complained that his health was deteriorating, and his girlfriend noticed that his vigor did appear to be waning, along with his romantic interest in her, but he was a sixty-four-year-old man, and that was to be expected. She did not see it as a precursor to murder, nor did anyone else. And yes, he had seen his personal wealth decline, but with a cool half million in the bank, he wasn't back on his heels. He was indebted to no one, the authorities said. If he had any grudges, he kept them to himself.

A month before the mass shooting, the couple checked into a room in the Mandalay Bay overlooking the venue that would soon become an abattoir, and his girlfriend thought it odd when she caught him staring blankly out the window, but not ominous. Why would she have? He had never been violent with her. He had been superior and demanding but had rarely, if ever, even uttered a harsh word to her—that wasn't his style. He hadn't telegraphed his intention to her in any way. Nor to anyone else. The term authorities use is "leakage." There was none.

And if she had happened to see any of his multiple laptops open and checked his browser history, what would she have found? Searches for music festivals in Chicago and Las Vegas. The Lollapalooza festival in Chicago; the Life Is Beautiful festival near the Ogden, a condominium in Las Vegas; and the Route 91 Harvest festival outside the Mandalay Bay. Even if she'd known that he had booked rooms overlooking all of those events—and he had, though he cancelled his reservation in Chicago—could she have predicted that he was looking for a site for a massacre? Or would she have just assumed that he was already moving on to his next obsessive hobby? Would anyone have guessed that when he rented a room at the Ogden, in what appears to have been a dress rehearsal for what was to come?

Would the killer have allowed them to?

If you peer deeply into the records gathered by the police and investigators, in hindsight you can see faint clues, the barest traces of the traits and the behaviors we've come to expect: the narcissism and selfishness, the grandiosity, the desire to be infamous, the obsession, the preparation. As his younger brother told investigators, even his suicide was an act of supreme narcissism, the final, selfish act of a man who "was bored with everything" and who, in a final act of grandiosity, would have wanted to slay as many people as he could "because he would want to be known as having the largest casualty count."[11]

But that was only clear in hindsight. After the fact.

We could not see that in advance.

In a terse, three-page document outlining its findings, the FBI's Behavioral Analysis Unit concluded that there was no single motive apart from, perhaps, a desire to kill the last killer. He was suicidal, but in his cruelty and narcissism he wanted to kill as many people as he could, driven by "a desire to attain . . . infamy."[12]

As Aaron Rouse, the special agent in charge of the FBI's Las Vegas office, told reporters when the document was released, "He acted alone. He committed a heinous act. He died by his own hand. If he wanted to leave a message, he would have left a message."[13]

But perhaps he did. Perhaps his obsessive desire to conceal his murderous intent, to scrub his methods clean of any familiar clues and hide his motives was a conscious attempt to magnify the horror and aggrandize himself. As researcher J. Reid Meloy tells me, "I think that the fact that we don't find any clearly stated motivation whatsoever was part of his plan."

Perhaps that was the message. Silence.

There is no silence on earth deeper than the silence between gunshots. It's terrifying. It's deafening. But it never lasts for long.

EPILOGUE

The Silence
between
Gunshots

AT A BUSINESS park in Edgewood, Maryland, and
a Walmart near Denver. Inside a church on a Sunday
morning in Sutherland Springs, and at Rancho Tehama
in California. At a car wash in Melcroft, Pennsylvania,
and in Parkland, Florida. At a veterans' home in
Yountville, California. Late at night at a Waffle House
in Nashville. And in the morning at a high school in
Santa Fe, Texas, where a cop could not save his own
mother. In the newsroom of the *Capital Gazette* in
Annapolis, Maryland. In Cincinnati and in Bakersfield,
California. At a warehouse in Perry, Maryland, and
at a synagogue in Pittsburgh on the Sabbath. At
the Borderline in Thousand Oaks, which had been
Tel Orfanos's refuge after surviving the atrocity in

Las Vegas. He was murdered at the Borderline, along with eleven others.

At a hospital in Chicago, at a bank in Sebring, Florida, and at a bar in State College, Pennsylvania. At a warehouse in Aurora, Illinois, and a municipal building in Virginia Beach.

At Gilroy. And El Paso, and Dayton, and Odessa.

One hundred and eighty-three innocent people dead in America. Two hundred and four wounded. And that's not even counting the dead and injured at places like the synagogue in Poway, California, where the death toll for whatever reason did not reach the perverse threshold we set for inclusion in the annals of atrocities. One woman died. Her name was Lori Gilbert-Kaye. Remember it. May her memory be a blessing. Nor does it include the fifty-one murders committed in Christchurch. Though it may have had American influences, it did not happen here.

As I write this, it is two years to the day since the mass public shooting at Las Vegas, and the body count continues to rise with no end in sight. Those twenty-four massacres listed above have all occurred since the silence after the gunshots settled on the crime scene in Las Vegas. Every one of those murders has been committed in the twenty-four months since I first began work on this book.[1] The silence is deep, and deafening, and it never lasts for very long.

It terrifies us, it taunts us, and the trauma is renewed with each new mass public shooting. It spreads like a poisonous fog until it touches every corner of the nation. It seems to paralyze us, leaving us frozen, unable to formulate any real response to it, unable to even agree on what it is that threatens us.

We search for easy answers. Tumors, video games, mental illness. Evil.

But there are no easy answers.

If anything has become clear in the decades since the

all-American boy next door climbed to the observation deck of the Tower in Austin and pulled the trigger to start the modern age of mass public shootings, if anything was made clear when the gambler climbed to the upper floors of a taller tower in Las Vegas, it's that there is no single silver bullet that will explain away all the lead and full metal–jacketed ones. There is no malignancy that we can spot on a CAT scan and excise with a scalpel. Or rather, if there is a malignancy, perhaps it's in all of us. Perhaps it's metastasized in a nation that, as sociologists Manning and Campbell tell us in chapter 1, has come to embrace "a culture of victimhood." Perhaps it resides, as studies show, in a culture that has come to prize fame—or infamy—above wealth or friendship.

If, as we've seen, those are among the traits that mass public shooters display, they are also among the traits we've come to display as a people. That's not to say that we're all potential killers. Certainly not. It's just to say that in the fog of war in peacetime, in a nation awash in easily obtained, high-powered, rapid-fire weapons and extended-round magazines, it can sometimes be difficult to spot with a casual glance the difference between a pair of middle-aged jokers cackling like schoolboys as they riddle targets with semiautomatic weapons fire at an Austin shooting range and real murderous schoolboys preparing for a holocaust in Colorado.

Difficult, but not impossible. As we saw in August 2019, after the summer of mass shootings during which we suffered and bled and died by the dozens in mass shootings in Gilroy, California; and in El Paso and Odessa in Texas; and in Dayton, Ohio, there are signs, signals, and portents that we can read, clear behavioral patterns that many of these killers follow in advance, which, if read correctly, can give us the tools we need to intervene with these potential killers before they commit an atrocity. It happened some forty times across the nation in

EPILOGUE

the aftermath of those massacres in the summer of 2019. Those arrests may have stopped a mass shooting. We'll never know for certain. It's also possible that they prevented one or more of the tens of thousands of suicides by gun recorded in this country annually, or one or more of the thousands upon thousands of other crimes of gun violence committed here each year. The warning signs are often the same. Learning to read the clues can save lives, and not just those of schoolchildren cowering in a supply closet or unsuspecting theatergoers on the opening night of the latest movie in the Batman franchise.

But as we saw in chapter 6, that kind of proactive response requires a high level of vigilance, and it remains an open question whether that level of high alert can be maintained when the initial shock and horror of a highly publicized mass shooting begins to fade, as it always does in our 24/7/365 mass-media culture, which focuses fiercely on an event or a series of events and then just as quickly moves on to cover the next big story.

Indeed, as we saw in chapter 9, in the silence that follows after the nomadic media moves on from an atrocity, or a string of them, often all that's left behind are the myths created in the fog of war in peacetime: the archetypes of the bad guy with the trench coat, the good guy with the gun. Or, as we discussed in chapter 2, we're left with the almost religious belief that somehow this isn't really about us as a people and instead represents some ancient Manichean struggle between the forces of good and the forces of evil. But as professor of rhetoric Rosa Eberly warns us, casting this epidemic as a battle of the elemental and eternal forces of good and evil risks letting us off the hook by falsely absolving us of our responsibility to, as that Bible on my shrink's bookshelf would have it, pluck the log out of our own eye.

To be sure, we have learned some valuable lessons, and they've been hard-earned. The media, of which I count myself a member, has recently made a valiant effort to deny these killers the fame—or infamy—so many of them crave. The electronic media particularly now generally chooses to focus on those killed or wounded in these atrocities, rather than aggrandizing the killers. But it may well be that in our desperate desire to find a cause, an explanation, a motive that will make sense of senseless shootings, we're still granting these murderers a measure of perverse celebrity when we publicize their manifestos or their social media postings aligning themselves with some dark movement. As we saw in chapter 4, there is indeed a malignancy of hatred and jealousy and rage that has taken root in some of the darker corners of our culture, and it has bubbled up to the surface. And it's become common in our public discourse to vent that impotent rage and to target the most vulnerable among us—immigrants, minorities, Jews, Muslims, gays, transgendered, lesbians.

Some of these murderers—the killer in Christchurch, the murderers at Mother Emanuel and at Tree of Life—feed on that pervasive rage and attach themselves to some perverse cause, in no small part to make themselves appear more important than they are. These manifestos and social media posts, these rants on 4chan and 8chan, may often just be a figurative version of Hamlet's inky cloak, a costume that barely conceals what they really are: the screeds of narcissistic killers.

Nor is it just the tales the killers tell us—and themselves—that we need to guard against. Myths are forged in the fog of war in peacetime, often innocently, and we in the media sometimes amplify those myths. When our corrections and clarifications come, they come too late. It is, as I wrote in chapter 9, often inadvertent and may at times be due to the frenetic nature of our news culture. As I've pored through countless media reports on mass public shootings while researching this book, I've come to the conclusion that it's a systemic problem and may have, at least in part, a systemic solution. If we accept that these mass killings are likely to continue—and it certainly seems as if we as a culture are prepared to surrender to that awful reality, at least for now—then national media outlets, either individually or collectively, might well consider establishing mass public shootings as a dedicated beat, assigning full-time reporters to a mass shooting desk, journalists trained for the purpose and experienced enough to at least recognize the myths we tell ourselves as *myths*.

Myths are as durable as diamonds. And they're found in abundance in our culture—the dark, silent places where our grudges spore, the places where narcissism and victimhood ooze together and become more toxic.

A culture that seems often to celebrate self-centered rage and antisocial grandiosity, a culture in which we're both hyperconnected and isolated from each other, is a culture that creates an environment that validates and inflames these killers and gives them places to hide. That is not likely to change overnight, or over years, or perhaps not even over the course of generations.

We are who we are, and we are who we have always been: a people capable of doing great things, of embracing and advancing the best human instincts. But we are also an angry, divided, fearful, and violent people, among the most violent nations on earth, as Lankford reminds us in chapter 1. We are a nation armed to the teeth, and as we discussed in chapter 8, there are among us decent, honorable, God-fearing people who believe in perfect faith that they have a divine ordinance to stockpile ordnance, including weapons originally designed to kill on the battlefield, and all the hundred-round drum magazines they desire.

It's not that they don't care about the rising body count. There are among them people like Stephen Willeford, the hero of Sutherland Springs, who care so deeply that they are willing to put their own lives on the line, stalking out barefoot to confront a killer on a Texas Sunday morning, and though they're rare, there are even a few, like Willeford, who say they would face that killer unarmed if they had to. As we've seen time and again in the wake of these atrocities, we are a nation that can conjure terrible villains, but we can also summon heroes like Willeford or like James Shaw Jr., who wrestled a rifle away from a deranged gunman barehanded, ending a mass public shooting at a Nashville Waffle House. The difference between those two men is not as great as one might imagine. One was a good guy with a gun. The other was a good guy without one. Both are American heroes, as was Tel Orfanos, the young sailor from California who, after dragging away the wounded during the Las Vegas massacre, died in hand-to-hand combat with another killer during the murders at the Borderline.

There are signs, of course, that many of us, a majority in fact, have decided that the time has come to wrestle the guns away from the killers. Yet we seem to lack the will or the faith to do so. As a Suffolk University poll of registered voters conducted in the bloody month of August 2019 found, 90 percent of the American people favored expanding background checks—including 90 percent of gun owners—and 69 percent of those polled would favor nationwide red-flag laws that would allow a judge to strip guns away from people adjudged dangerous. Nearly 60 percent supported the idea of banning extended magazines.[2]

The devil, of course, is in the details. Expanded background checks—like the law proposed after the Sandy Hook murders by Sen. Pat Toomey, a Pennsylvania Republican, and Sen. Joe Manchin, a West Virginia Democrat, which would have required background checks at gun shows but not between private sellers—would not have stopped the killer at Odessa, for example, from buying his semiautomatic rifle. Though a background check at a gun shop discovered a history of mental illness and a series of encounters with law enforcement and thus barred him from buying his rifle, there is still no law on the books that would have prevented him from buying the weapon from a private seller with no background check at all. Nor would any combination of red-flag laws or background checks have stopped the killer in Las Vegas from amassing the arsenal he used to commit the single worst mass public shooting by a lone gunman in the nation's long and bloody history. That secretive, generally nondescript killer had carefully covered his tracks, making perfectly sure that he would trigger no alarms. Nor would they have stopped the killer at Sandy Hook, whose mother had legally purchased the weapons he used first to murder her and then to murder twenty children and six adults at an elementary school.

It's perhaps in recognition of that fact, according to the Suffolk poll, that a majority of Americans support a return to some version of the assault weapons ban, which was the law from 1994 until 2004, when it was allowed to lapse. It's worth noting that the law, which banned the sale and importation of certain semiautomatic weapons, did nothing to remove the millions of such guns already in circulation; thus it was comparatively easy for the Columbine killers to acquire a TEC-9, a banned handgun, through a straw purchase at a gun show.

It would be a tall order in this divided nation to craft a version of the assault weapons ban that would include a mandatory buyback, as New Zealand did when it was rocked by the massacre at Christchurch. For evidence of how fraught such an effort would be, you need look no further than the confrontation between two Texans at the beginning of the Democratic presidential primary race for 2020, when former state representative Beto O'Rourke, then a presidential hopeful angered by the twin mass shootings in El Paso and Odessa, insisted that he would indeed as president move to enact a mandatory buyback and confiscate the weapons of those who did not comply. That prompted a Republican state lawmaker to post a challenge—or perhaps a threat—on Twitter: "My AR is ready for you."[3]

It would be easy to dismiss the exchange as preening, perhaps on both of their parts, but in many regards the confrontation between the two men cast in high relief the deep chasm between Americans over the issue of gun control.

Indeed, that seemingly bottomless, unbridgeable chasm between Americans on opposite sides of the gun-control debate appears to have grown only wider and deeper in recent years as the body count has risen ever more dramatically. And for many Americans, it seems, a sense of hopelessness has taken hold. It's no surprise then that despite our calls for tougher regulations on extended-round magazines and bans of semiautomatic rifles, despite our apparent faith in expanded background checks and red-flag laws, the American people remain grimly pessimistic about the possibility that our elected officials will do anything to enact these measures. Sixty-eight percent of the voters queried told pollsters in that August 2019 poll that they believed it unlikely that Congress would pass any significant legislation in the year before the next presidential election. And they seem to have been right. Bills that would dramatically expand background checks to include private sales, a revived assault weapons ban, and a bill that demands that specific semiautomatic rifles be licensed (thus making it arguably less likely that they would slip into the wrong hands), as well as other attempts to address the issue, have all languished in a kind of political limbo. Even those measures that have passed the US House of Representatives are unable to even get a hearing in the Senate.

None of them, of course, would prevent every death or stop every mass shooter. From the days of Tom Quick and the Paxton Boys to the modern-day massacre at Odessa, we are and always have been a violent people. But some lives would doubtlessly be saved. "Whosoever saves a single soul," the ancient Jewish sages wrote in the Talmud, is "ascribed [merit] . . . as though he had preserved a complete world."

And yet we have remained largely silent, lost in the fog of war in peacetime.

As the Suffolk poll indicates, however, there are signs that pressure may finally be mounting to break that silence. A month after the Parkland massacre, tens of thousands of demonstrators gathered in the nation's capital for the March for Our Lives protest. It was a massive rally organized largely through social media, in effect turning the same electronic sword that many killers use to stoke their rage and reinforce their murderous impulses into a digital plowshare. There were similar rallies across the country. In what will be remembered as the most poignant moment of the rally, survivor Emma González, then a senior at Parkland, stepped to the podium, and in a quavering voice, spoke for about two minutes, simply reciting the names of her friends who had been murdered and adding a few touching details about them.[4]

And then she fell silent. For four minutes and twenty-six seconds that seemed to last an eternity, she stood, tears streaming down her cheeks, as thousands at the protest in Washington and countless others who saw her on television fell silent with her. It was a heart-wrenchingly powerful memorial for the murdered, for the wounded, yes. But it was more than that. It was a mirror held up to America, an indictment and a challenge, a wordless call to feel the crushing weight of all the terrifying silences between all the deadly gunshots fired since August 1, 1966, and to find the will and the courage to finally break that silence.

Her silence was our silence. Emma González's silence ended that day with these words: "Fight for your lives, before it's someone else's job."

Her silence was broken. Ours has not yet been.

ACKNOWLEDGMENTS

HE DIDN'T EVEN bother to look up when I walked through the front door that morning. He just stood there, dispassionately studying the shards of glass that littered the lobby of the headquarters of the little weekly paper on the Jersey Shore that he had started from nothing twenty years earlier. A slight breeze wafted in through the jagged hole where the front window used to be and carried the pale blue smoke from his Chesterfield King deeper into the building.

"Another satisfied reader?" I asked.

"You know what really pisses me off about this?" he said as he lightly tapped the brick that had shattered the window with the tip of his shiny black Italian-made loafer.

"What?"

"The fact that you didn't write anything this week to deserve this," he said.

It's been thirty-five years or so since my old friend, boss, and mentor Dave Thaler gave me that crash course on what it means to be a journalist, and though he's been gone for nearly twenty—the Chesterfields finally did him in—his ghost has loomed large for me as I worked on this project. The way Dave saw things, awards and accolades and even advertising revenue were all well and good, but a journalist wasn't really doing his or her job unless they grabbed hold of an electrified issue with both hands, consequences be damned, and held on until somebody cried uncle.

And if somebody somewhere got angry or upset enough to toss a brick through your window, that wasn't a tragedy or a line on an insurance claim form, in his estimation. It was the highest praise that one of the journalists who worked for him could receive. It was, as he saw it, the whole reason he became a newspaperman in the first place—it was what drove him to gamble everything he had and everything he could borrow to build the old *Bayshore Independent*.

I have no idea whether the reporting in this book is going to prompt that kind of anger from any of its readers. It may not. But it ought to. The roots of this deadly epidemic of mass public shootings—which has killed nearly two thousand Americans over the last five decades and counting—run deep in this culture, and there will certainly be those who see any exploration of it as an attack on their interests and their values.

It didn't take any courage at all to write this book. But it took immense courage, in our hyperdivided and angry country, to publish it. And that's why I need to express my deepest gratitude to the remarkable people at the University of Texas Press who were willing, against all odds, to take a chance on producing this book, knowing that there was a very good chance that it would provoke outrage among some, and worse, indifference among others.

There is no publishing house in the country that I would rather have at my back on a project like this than the University of Texas Press. Every member of the team is a remarkable person and a consummate professional. I've worked with quite a few editors in my life, but not one of them could trick me into raising my game better than Casey Kittrell, a guy who could launch a thousand words with the equivalent of a verbal shrug of his shoulders. Whatever weaknesses this book might have, they're all my own. Whatever strengths it has, you can give the credit to Casey. And to Paul Wade, who challenged me repeatedly and rightly on both form and substance. And to the gimlet-eyed copyediting of Leslie Tingle under the guidance of Lynne Ferguson and her team. Every writer should be lucky enough to get a chance to work with people of their caliber.

Because UTP is a university press, there are levels of review that this book faced that the average writer for a major trade publisher never gets to experience. And I could not be more grateful for that. Indeed, I am in the debt of the blind readers Casey assembled to poke holes in this project before it went to print. They challenged me to better articulate my thesis, and they helped me rein in my periodic excesses. This book, while still far from perfect, is far better because of them.

One other thing that UTP has that no other publisher in the country can boast is Gianna LaMorte. This is my third book for the press. Gianna willed both of those prior books into existence, and she was the driving force behind this one. She's been a patron, a muse, and a friend, and of those three, I'm most honored by the last of them.

Beyond the walls of the University of Texas, this book

also benefited from the wisdom and generosity of experts and scholars, people like Rosa Eberly, now at Penn State University, and her former student, Brad Serber, most recently at the University of North Dakota, both of whom I now consider friends; and others, like Casey Kelly at the University of Nebraska and Adam Lankford at the University of Alabama. Each of them has grappled with the issues raised by the reporting in this book, and their hard-earned wisdom and their selfless willingness to share it has been invaluable.

There are some, who because of their association with law enforcement, prefer to remain anonymous, and I will respect that. They know who they are. And I hope they know how deeply indebted I am to them.

I also need to thank my old friend and colleague Corky Siemaszko, whom I can describe without fear of serious contradiction as the single best rewrite man who ever lived for permitting me to bounce enough raw copy off him to gag a mullet and never once losing patience with me.

I owe a debt to Michael Stamps and Craig Stutman and Dave Snyder at Delaware Valley University, who early in this process opened their doors to me and provided a forum where I could hash out some of the themes in this book with some very engaged and insightful students.

And I need to thank my wife, Kren, and my children, Liam, Seneca, Yona, and Miriam, for their patience and their support. It's one thing to choose to immerse yourself in the horrors that are detailed in this book; it's quite another to be subjected to it because it's daddy's job. They've all handled the challenge with a level of grace that has made me both grateful and proud.

During the two years that I spent reporting this book, I often had friends reach out to me, wondering how I was coping with the stress of focusing constantly, day in and day out, on the details of mass murder. I was and remain touched by their concern. I know they meant well, but if

I'm to be perfectly honest, I also found their questions about my emotional state to be misplaced. I was never anything more than a chronicler of other people's pain. And on those occasions when it did become too painful, I took strength from the courage of those who have been touched by this epidemic. I reminded myself that I have not earned the right to claim their suffering as my own.

And sometimes, I cried.

Which leads me to my final note of thanks, though I know that no thanks can ever be sufficient. I am in utter awe of those people who have been touched by these atrocities over the years, who have experienced the unimaginable pain of surviving a mass public shooting, or who have lost loved ones to this epidemic and yet still had the courage and grace and faith to spend time talking to me.

Every one of them is, in my mind, a hero. As I said in the beginning of this book, this story is their story.

I'm humbled that they allowed me to tell it. And I will be forever grateful to each and every one of them for that.

NOTES

PROLOGUE

1. Martinez's account is based on interviews with the author, an account he gave in "Out of the Blue," by the *Texas Standard* (2016), and his personal essay, "For Whom the Tower Chimes," published on tower-shooting.com in 2016.

2. Much of Claire Wilson James's account is based on the author's interview with her. Additional material was drawn from Pamela Colloff's "The Reckoning: The Story of Claire Wilson," *Texas Monthly*, March 2016.

3. Gary Lavergne, *A Sniper in the Tower* (Denton: University of North Texas Press, 1997), prologue, "Weathered Metal Plaques."

4. "Tom Quick and the Pioneers of the Delaware," *Wayne County* (PA) *Herald*, March 20, 1851.

CHAPTER 1

The Texas Sharpshooter Fallacy

1. US Public Health Service, *Vital Statistics of the United States, 1966*, vol. 2, Mortality, Section 1, p. 234.

2. The medical aspects are discussed in *Report on the Charles J. Whitman Catastrophe*, Texas Governor's Committee and Consultants, Archives and Information Services Division, Texas State Library and Archives Commission, Austin.

3. The number is based on the *Washington Post* editorial "54 Years, 165 Mass Shootings, 1,196 Dead," August 11, 2019; and Guide to Mass Shootings in America, 1982–2020 (database), *Mother Jones*, which added seven dead in the August 31, 2019, mass shooting in Odessa-Midland, Texas, motherjones.com/politics/2012/12/mass-shootings-mother-jones-full-data/.

4. *2017 Crime in the United States*, Criminal Justice Information Services Division, table 1, https://ucr.fbi.gov/crime-in-the-u.s/2017; and CDC, National Vital Statistics Report (NVSS), 2017, table B, 6.

5. Franklin E. Zimring and Gordon Hawkins, *Crime Is Not the Problem: Lethal Violence in America* (New York: Oxford University Press, 1999).

6. *2017 Crime in the United States*, Expanded Homicide Data, table 7, https://ucr.fbi.gov/crime-in-the-u.s/2017.

7. CDC, NVSS, 2017, table 6, "Number of Deaths by Selective Causes," 35.

8. Aaron Karp, "Estimating Global Civilian Held Firearms Numbers," briefing paper, Small Arms Survey, June 2018, table 1, p. 4, www.smallarmssurvey.org.

9. Tom W. Smith and Jaesok Son, *General Social Survey Final Report: Trends in Gun Ownership in the United States, 1972–2014*, National Opinion Research Center (NORC), University of Chicago, March 2015.

10. "Modern Sporting Rifle Production Plus Imports Less Exports," *Firearms Production in the United States* (2015 ed.), Industry Intelligence Reports, National Shooting Sports Foundation, 5.

11. Alex Yablon, "How Many Assault Weapons Do Americans Own?," thetrace.org, September 22, 2018.

12. *2017 Crime in the United States*, Expanded Homicide Data, table 19, https://ucr.fbi.gov/crime-in-the-u.s/2017.

13. Elzerie de Jager, Eric Goralnik, and Justin C. McCarty, "Lethality of Civilian Active Shooter Incidents with and without Semiautomatic Rifles in the United States," *JAMA*, September 11, 2018.

14. *2017 Crime in the United States*, Expanded Homicide Data, table 11, https://ucr.fbi.gov/crime-in-the-u.s/2017.

15. "Firearms Commerce in the United States, Annual Statistical Update 2018," US Department of Justice, Bureau of Alcohol, Tobacco, Firearms and Explosives, Exhibit 1, Firearms Manufactured (1986–2016), 1, atf.gov.resource-center/docs.

16. Dylan Matthews, "Caliber, Cartridges and Bump Stocks: Guns Explained for Non-Gun People," *Vox*, September 4, 2019. Also see Consumer Federation of America, "America's Gun Industry," https://consumerfed.org/pdfs/industry.pdf.

17. Michael Kosnar and Pete Williams, "Pandemic Pushes U.S. Gun Sales to All-Time High," NBCnews.com, April 3, 2020.

18. Adam Lankford, "Public Mass Shooters and Firearms: A Cross-National Study of 171 Countries," *Violence and Victims* 31.2 (2016): 9.

19. Bradley Campbell and Jason Manning, *The Rise of Victimhood Culture: Microaggressions, Safe Spaces, and the New Culture Wars* (Cham, Switzerland: Palgrave Macmillan, 2018).

20. "How Young People View Their Lives, Future and Politics: A Portrait of 'Generation Next,'" Pew Research Center, January 9, 2007, http://assets.pewresearch.org/wp-content/uploads/sites/3/2010/10/300.pdf.

21. The Violence Project, Mass Shooter Database, United States, 1966–2019, https://www.theviolenceproject.org/mass-shooter-database/.

22. "Elliot Rodger's Retribution," transcript, *Los Angeles Times*, May 24, 2014.

23. Violence Project, Mass Shooter Database, theviolenceproject.org /mass-shooter-database/.

CHAPTER 2

Deliver Us from Evil

1. Joan Chittister, "What Kind of People Are These?," *National Catholic Reporter*, October 9, 2006.

2. Julia Spicher Kasdorf, "To Pasture: 'Amish Forgiveness,' Silence, and the West Nickel Mines School Shooting," *CrossCurrents* 59.2 (2007).

3. Patrick Burns, "Book Details 'Amish Forgiveness' after Nickel Mines Shooting," *Lancaster Online*, June 5, 2007.

4. Frank Bruni, "Bush Blames 'a Wave of Evil' for Shootings across Nation," *New York Times*, September 17, 1999.

5. Dave Cullen, *Columbine* (New York: Hachette Book Group, 2009), 287.

6. Cullen, 224.

7. "Pilpul" is defined by *Merriam-Webster* as "critical analysis and hairsplitting : casuistic argumentation, especially among Jewish scholars on talmudic subjects."

8. Rosa A. Eberly, "Deliver Ourselves from 'Evil,'" *Rhetoric and Public Affairs* 6.3 (Fall 2003): 552.

9. Grant Duwe, "Actually, There Is a Clear Link between Mass Shootings and Mental Illness," *Los Angeles Times*, February 23, 2018.

10. Guide to Mass Shootings in America (database), motherjones. com/politics/2012/12/mass-shootings-mother-jones-full-data/.

11. Linda Teplin, Gary McClelland, Karen Abram, et al., "Crime Victimization in Adults with Severe Mental Illness: Comparison with the National Crime Victimization Survey," *JAMA*, August 2005.

12. Kevin Sack, "Trial Documents Show Dylann Roof Had Mental Disorders," *New York Times*, February 2, 2017.

13. "Landmark Survey Reports on the Prevalence of Personality Disorders in the United States," NIH/National Institute on Alcohol Abuse and Alcoholism, August 3, 2004.

14. Source, Facts, and Statistics, Anxiety and Depression Association of America, https://adaa.org/about-adaa/press-room/facts-statistics.

15. Data and Statistics on Autism Spectrum Disorder, Centers for Disease Control and Prevention, cdc.gov/ncbddd/autism/data.html.

16. Tom Zoellner, *A Safeway in Arizona: What the Gabrielle Giffords*

Shooting Tells Us about the Grand Canyon State and Life in America (New York: Viking, 2011).

17. Heatly's report is reprinted in *Tower Sniper: The Terror of America's First Active Shooter on Campus*, by Monte Akers, Nathan Akers, and Richard Friedman (John M. Hardy Publishing, 2016).

18. Virginia Tech Review Panel, *Mass Shootings at Virginia Tech, April 16, 2007: Report of the Review Panel presented to Governor Kaine, Commonwealth of Virginia*, 35.

19. Virginia Tech Review Panel.

20. Virginia Tech Review Panel, 42.

21. Virginia Tech Review Panel, 47.

22. Donald Kraybill, Steven M. Nolt, and David L. Weaver-Zercher, *Amish Grace: How Forgiveness Transcended Tragedy* (San Francisco: Jossey Bass, 2010.)

23. *Report of the State's Attorney for the Judicial District of Danbury on the Shootings at Sandy Hook Elementary School and 36 Yogananda Street, Newtown, Connecticut on Dec. 14, 2012*, p. 26, https://portal. ct.gov/-/media/DCJ/SandyHookFinalReportpdf.pdf.

CHAPTER 3

To Kill the Last Killer

1. "Soul Has Weight, Physician Thinks," *New York Times*, March 11, 1907.

2. Office of the Child Advocate of the State of Connecticut, *Shooting at Sandy Hook Elementary School: Report of the Office of the Child Advocate*, November 21, 2014, p. 38, ct.gov/oca/lib/oca/sandy hook11212014.pdf.

3. Office of the Child Advocate of the State of Connecticut, 15.

4. Office of the Child Advocate of the State of Connecticut, 16.

5. Office of the Child Advocate of the State of Connecticut, 18.

6. Office of the Child Advocate of the State of Connecticut, 25.

7. Office of the Child Advocate of the State of Connecticut, 25.

8. Office of the Child Advocate of the State of Connecticut, 29.

9. Office of the Child Advocate of the State of Connecticut, 37.

10. Office of the Child Advocate of the State of Connecticut, 49.

11. Office of the Child Advocate of the State of Connecticut, 39.

12. Office of the Child Advocate of the State of Connecticut, 50.

13. Matthew Lysiak, *Newtown: An American Tragedy* (New York: Gallery Books, 2013), 24.

14. FBI Records, Sandy Hook Elementary School Shooting, released October 24, 2017, https://vault.fbi.gov/sandy-hook-elementary-school -shooting.

15. FBI Records, Sandy Hook Elementary School Shooting.

16. Akers, Akers, and Friedman, *Tower Sniper*, 267.

CHAPTER 4

"'Tis Not Alone My Inky Cloak"

1. Terrie Morgan-Besecker and David Singleton, "Eric Frein Infatuated with Serbian Military," *Scranton Times-Tribune*, October 12, 2014.

2. *United States v. Robert Bowers*, Criminal No. 18-292, superseding indictment filed in the US District Court for the Western District of Pennsylvania, January 29, 2019.

3. Daniel Zwerdling, "Walter Reed Officials Asked: Was Hasan Psychotic?," NPR.org, November 11, 2009.

4. Adam Lankford, *The Myth of Martyrdom: What Really Drives Suicide Bombers, Rampage Shooters, and Other Self-Destructive Killers* (New York: St. Martin's Press, 2013), 93.

5. Paula Chin, "A Texas Massacre," *People*, November 4, 1991.

6. *A Ticking Time Bomb: Counterterrorism Lessons from the U.S. Government's Failure to Prevent the Fort Hood Attack*, special report from Senate Committee on Homeland Security and Governmental Affairs, February 2011.

7. Dana Priest, "Fort Hood Suspect Warned of Threats within the Ranks," *Washington Post*, November 10, 2009.

8. David Johnson and Scott Shane, "U.S. Knew of Suspect's Ties to Radical Cleric," *New York Times*, November 9, 2009.

9. Sudarsan Raghavan, "Cleric Says He Was Confidant to Hasan," *Washington Post*, November 16, 2009.

10. Tessa Berensen, "Isis Tells Followers It's 'Easy' to Get Firearms from U.S. Gun Shows," *Time*, May 5, 2017.

11. Casey Ryan Kelly, *Apocalypse Man: The Death Drive and the Rhetoric of White Masculine Victimhood* (Columbus: Ohio State University Press, 2020), 2.

12. Sigmund Freud, *Civilization and Its Discontents* (New York: Norton, 1961), 58.

13. Rich Lord, "How Robert Bowers Went from Conservative to White Nationalist," *Pittsburgh Post-Gazette*, November 10, 2018.

14. William Wan, Annie Gowan, and Tim Craig, "Pittsburgh Shooting Suspect Left Fleeting Impression in Neighborhoods He Lived in for Decades," *Washington Post*, October 21, 2018.

15. 2017 Audit of Anti-Semitic Incidents, ADL, adl.org/resources /reports/2017-audit-of-anti-semitic-incidents#themes-and-trends-.

16. "Rockne Newell Pleads Guilty to Killing 3, Gets Three Life Sentences," Associated Press, May 30, 2015.

17. Lord, "Bowers from Conservative to White Nationalist."
18. Lankford, *Myth of Martyrdom*, 114.

<small>CHAPTER 5</small>
Jokers Wild

1. Timothy Johnson, "Alex Jones and Roger Stone Visited a Gun Range to Prepare for Civil War If Trump Is Removed from Office," Media Matters for America, December 21, 2017, mediamatters.org/alex-jones/alex-jones-and-roger-stone-visited-gun-range-prepare-civil-war-if-trump-removed-office.

2. Nancy Gibbs and Timothy Roche, "The Columbine Tapes," *Time*, December 20, 1999.

3. Dave Cullen, "The Reluctant Killer," *Guardian*, April 24, 2009.

4. Samantha Henig, "Q&A: A Campus Shooter Talks About VA Tech," *Newsweek*, May 1, 2007.

5. Subsequent Parole Consideration Hearing, State of California Parole Board Hearings, In the matter of the Life Term Parole Consideration Hearing of: Brenda Spencer, September 7, 2016, p. 44, https://schoolshooters.info/sites/default/files/Spencer_Parole_Hearing_2009.pdf.

6. Videotaped deposition of Mitchell Johnson taken on behalf of the plaintiffs at the Washington County Courthouse . . . Monday, April 2, 2007, p. 21, YouTube.

7. David Koon, "Westside Killer Seeks Handgun Permit, State Police to Golden: No," *Arkansas Times*, December 11, 2008; and Elisha Fieldstadt, "Arkansas School Shooter Who Killed Five in 1998 Dies in Head-On Crash," NBCnews.com, July 29, 2019.

<small>CHAPTER 6</small>
If You See Something, Say Something

1. *State of Indiana v. Mary York*, case number 89D01-1910-F5-000113, filed 10/11/2019, mycase.IN.gov.

2. James Silver, Andre Simons, and Sara Craun, *A Study of the Pre-Attack Behaviors of Active Shooters in the United States between 2000 and 2013*, FBI, US Department of Justice, June 2018, fbi.gov/file-repository/pre-attack-behaviors-of-active-shooters-in-us-2000-2013.pdf/view.

3. Juliana Menasce Howowitz, "How Male and Female Gun Owners in the U.S. Compare," Pew Research Center, June 29, 2017, pewresearch.org/fact-tank/2017/06/29/how-male-and-female-gun-owners-in-the-u-s-compare/.

4. Guide to Mass Shootings in America, motherjones.com/politics/2012/07/mass-shootings-map/.

5. Silver, Simons, and Craun, *Study of Pre-Attack Behaviors, 2000–2013*.

6. *Protecting America's Schools: A U.S. Secret Service Analysis of Targeted School Violence*, US Department of Homeland Security, USSS Threat Assessment Center, November 2019, p. 21.

7. Volusia County Sheriff's Office Incident Report on Tristan Scott Wix, agency report number 190017597, filed August 16, 2019.

8. *Study of Pre-Attack Behaviors*, 24, fbi.gov/file-repository/pre-attack-behaviors-of-active-shooters-in-us-2000-2013.pdf/view.

CHAPTER 7

A Good Guy with a Gun

1. Ray Martinez, *Out of the Blue*, a Texas Standard documentary, https://towerhistory.org/profiles/ray-martinez/.

2. "A Study of Active Shooters Incidents in the United States, 2000–2013"; "Active Shooter Incidents in the United States, 2014–2015"; and "Active Shooter Incidents in the United States in 2018," fbi.gov/resources/library.

3. "Active Shooter Incidents, 2000–2013," fbi.gov/resources/library.

4. "Active Shooter Incidents 2018," fbi.gov/resources/library.

5. Herman Wong, "James Shaw Jr. on Why He Rushed the Waffle House Shooter: 'He Was Going to Have to Work to Kill Me,'" *Washington Post*, April 22, 2018.

6. Holly Yan, "Teacher Who Tackled Gunman Speaks Out for the First Time Since Getting Shot," CNN.com, May 29, 2018.

7. Tallahassee Police Department Field Case Report Supplement, Case # 2018-00034992.

8. Phillip M. Bailey and Alison Ross, "'Whites Don't Shoot Whites': What One Man Says Kroger Shooter Told Him," *Louisville Courier Journal*, October 25, 2018.

9. Christal Hayes, "Armed Citizen Who Shot Oklahoma Gunman Told Worried Crowd, 'I'm Here to Help,'" *USA Today*, May 25, 2018.

10. Meg Wingerter and Elise Schmelzer, "STEM School Highlands Ranch Didn't Know Security Guard Who Shot Student Was Armed," *Denver Post*, August 27, 2019.

11. Christian Martinez, "Officer Killed in Thousand Oaks Shooting Killed by Friendly Fire," *USA Today*, December 7, 2018.

12. Kathleen Wilson, "Thousand Oaks Shooter Died of Self-Inflicted Gunshot Wound at Borderline, Autopsy Shows," *Ventura County Star*, November 10, 2018.

13. Richard Gonzales, "Coroner Says Gilroy Festival Shooter Killed Himself, Contradicts Police Reports," NPR.org, August 2, 2019.

14. Adeel Hassan, "Dayton Gunman Shot 26 People in 32 Seconds, Police Timeline Reveals," *New York Times*, August 13, 2019.

15. S. L. A. Marshall, *Men Against Fire: The Problem of Battle Command* (Norman: University of Oklahoma Press, 2000), 57.

16. Dave Grossman and Bruce K. Siddle, "Psychological Effects of Combat," in *Encyclopedia of Violence, Peace, and Conflict* (San Diego: Academic Press, 2000).

17. *Marjory Stoneman Douglas High School Public Safety Commission, Initial Report*, January 2, 2019, p. 96, http://www.fdle.state.fl.us/MSDHS /CommissionReport.pdf.

CHAPTER 8

I Cling to My Gun, You Cling to Yours

1. Andy Mehalshick (with Jayne Ann Bugda), "I-Team Special Report: Preparing for Doomsday," WYOU/WBRE, February 7, 2017, https://www .pahomepage.com/news/i-team-special-report-preparing-for-doomsday/.

2. Tara Isabella Burton, "The Cultlike Church behind a Ceremony with AR-15s and Bullet Crowns Explained," *Vox*, March 1, 2018, https://www .vox.com/2018/3/1/17067894/church-bullet-crowns-ar15-world-peace -unification-sanctuary-moonies-moon.

3. In its January 2, 2019, report to the governor, the Marjory Stoneman Douglas High School Public Safety Commission describes the circumstances of Feis's murder as follows: "While Feis himself was not seen opening that door, a flood of sunlight entered the stairwell at 2:23:25. Simultaneously, Cruz entered the stairwell from the door separating the stairwell and the west end of the first floor so that Cruz was immediately facing Feis. Cruz raised the rifle and fired thereby fatally wounding Feis. Feis would later be found immediately outside of the exterior west stairwell door. It is unknown why Feis did not call a Code Red after being told by a student that there was someone with a gun inside Building 12" (*MSDHS Initial Report*, 64).

4. Twitter thread, @RepMattSchaefer, August 31, 2019, https://twitter .com/repmattschaefer/status/1167989160507895809?lang=en.

5. *District of Columbia v. Heller*, decided June 26, 2008, Scalia, 7, p. 10.

6. *District of Columbia v. Heller*.

7. *District of Columbia v. Heller*, syllabus, p. 2.

8. *Holy Spirit Association for the Unification of World Christianity v. World Peace and Unification Sanctuary, Inc.*, filed in US District Court, Middle District of Pennsylvania, July 30, 2018.

9. Kate Shellnut, "Packing in the Pews: The Connection Between God and Guns," *Christianity Today*, November 8, 2017.

10. Fox contributor Pastor Robert Jeffers, *Fox and Friends*, November 6, 2017, https://video.foxnews.com/v/5636739415001/?playlist_id= 2114913880001#sp=show-clips/daytime.

11. Shullnut, "Packing in the Pews."

12. Rich Lowry, "Yes, Gun Ownership Is a God-Given Right," *National Review*, September 6, 2019.

13. Daniel Flatley, "Air Force's Repeated Errors Let Sutherland Springs Shooter Buy Firearms," Bloomberg.com, December 6, 2018.

CHAPTER 9

The Fog of War in Peacetime

1. Abe Aboraya, "Five First Responders to the Pulse Massacre, One Diagnosis: PTSD," WFME/ProPublica, June 11, 2018.

2. Jaclyn V. Schildkraut, "Mass Murder and the Mass Media: An Examination of the Media Discourse on U.S. Rampage Shootings, 2000–2012," unpublished diss., Texas State University, San Marcos, 2014.

3. "54 Years, 165 Mass Shootings," *Washington Post*.

4. Aboraya, "Five First Responders."

5. Bessel A. van der Kolk, *The Body Keeps the Score: Brain, Mind, and Body in the Healing of Trauma* (New York: Penguin, 2015), 1.

6. Madeline Will, "'I Worry Every Day': Lockdown Drills Prompt Fear, Self-Reflection after School Shooting," *Education Week*, February 20, 2018.

7. Marjory Stoneman Douglas High School Public Safety Commission Timeline (animated), compiled by the Florida Department of Law Enforcement, http://www.fdle.state.fl.us/MSDHS/Timeline.aspx.

8. Steven Rich and John Woodrow Cox, "What If Someone Was Shooting?," *Washington Post*, December 26, 2018.

9. Erika Christakis, "Active Shooter Drills Are Tragically Misguided," *Atlantic*, March 2019.

10. Justine Lofton, "$48 Million Dollar High School Designed to Thwart Active Shooters," *Michigan Live*, September 4, 2019, https://www.mlive.com/news/2019/09/48m-michigan-high-school-designed-to-thwart-active-shooters.html.

11. Pew Research Center Survey of U.S. teens ages 13–17, conducted March 7–April 10, 2018.

12. van der Kolk, *Body Keeps the Score*, 1.

CHAPTER 10

From a Taller Tower

1. Las Vegas Metropolitan Police Department Voluntary Statement, Event No. 171001-3519, released to the public May 2018, p. 44.

2. LVMPD Criminal Investigative Report of 1 October Mass Casualty Shooting, LVMPD Event No. 171001-3519, released August 3, 2018, p. 20.

3. "Key Findings of the Behavioral Analysis Unit's Las Vegas Review Panel," US Department of Justice, FBI, January 2019, p. 1, https://www.hsdl.org/?abstract&did=820782.

4. LVMPD Report of 1 October Mass Casualty Shooting, 113.

5. LVMPD Report of 1 October Mass Casualty Shooting, 89.

6. LVMPD Report of 1 October Mass Casualty Shooting, 52.

7. LVMPD Report of 1 October Mass Casualty Shooting, 111.

8. Sabrina Tavernise, Serge F. Kovaleski, and Julie Turkewitz, "Who Was Stephen Paddock? The Mystery of a Non-Descript 'Numbers Guy,'" *New York Times*, October 7, 2017.

9. Adam Geller, Michael Balsamo, and Jonathan Cooper, "He Was the King of Microagression," Associated Press, October 6, 2017.

10. Silver, Simons, and Craun, *Pre-Attack Behaviors of Active Shooters.*

11. LVMPD Report of 1 October Mass Casualty Shooting, 116.

12. "Key Findings of the Las Vegas Review Panel," 2.

13. "Vegas Gunman Stephen Paddock Inspired by Criminal Father's Reputation," Associated Press, January 29, 2019.

EPILOGUE

The Silence between Gunshots

1. Guide to Mass Shootings in America (database), motherjones.com /politics/2012/07/mass-shootings-map/.

2. "90% of Registered Voters Want Firearms Background Checks," Suffolk University/USA Today poll, September 9, 2019.

3. "Briscoe Cain Says His 'My AR Is Ready for You' Tweet Benefited Him, Beto O'Rourke," *Texas Tribune*, September 28, 2019.

4. Louis Lucero II, "What Emma Gonzalez Said without Words at the March for Our Lives Rally," *New York Times*, March 24, 2018.

INDEX